dedication

To Chelsea and Cady for unleashing the muses with their divine spirits; you are everything that is beautiful in this world. To Bill, who showed me the sound of one hand clapping; in watching you, I've learned to be brave every day and in the face of every obstacle. Special thanks to Mava, whose creativity can't be contained and spills out into all areas of life. To Kerri, Todd, and Randy; you are all practitioners of the creative life, and I am proud to be on this journey with you.

Finally, my deepest gratitude to the talented souls at Interweave, including: Tricia Waddell whose vision jump-started this journey; designer Karla Baker who lent her sublime hand; and especially project editor Darlene D'Agostino who remained cheerful during the brutal process of transforming a pile of words into a real book. Her gypsy magic saved the day. For Pokey Bolton, who inspires everyday artists worldwide and still finds time to rock.

Personal note: This book was a necessary exercise for me. With the support of so many friends near and far, I've planted and nurtured a garden of creativity in my soul. The constant blossoming of colorful ideas has been possible only through my interaction with a host of wonderful, inspirational people. Like anything worthwhile, creativity improves with practice. A number of online groups bringing global artists together have been the impetus for so much of my practice. Wherever you are, you can find kindred souls for learning, experimenting, and trading the work of your hands. I encourage you to connect with this great circle of artists. It will be an amazing source of inspiration. They have pushed me to grow and learn continually. My mailbox has hosted an exciting carnival of treasures, and I remain eternally indebted to those artful spirits who have shared so freely their precious gifts.

MIXED-MEDIA PAPER-CLOTH
INVITING SERENDIPITY

I love the concept of serendipity papers—you can create magic without intention, without even considering complementary colors. There's no forethought, no natural selection. Just cover your work surface with a protective piece of paper and create away. As you clean up after your project, there lies a curious melding of the paint, the stamping and inks, and the bits of evidence left from the previous project. Cut this palette into squares, and each is unique and interesting. The resulting blocks resemble part of a larger whole because words, images, and colors move off the edge of the page. It's like you are capturing a small sampling of the universe.

These little luck-struck creations made me wonder if you can encourage serendipity: Can you increase the odds that something magical and creative will happen in your studio? So I began to make serendipity papers outside of the traditional, leave-it-all-up-to-fate method. What did I discover? Serendipity can be created. It does not have to exist as just a by-product of other endeavors.

This book is for both collage artists and quilters who want to expand their options by entering the world of mixed media. Many books exist for paper artists and an equal number for the quilter and fiber artist, but few show how to cross mediums and blend the surface design versatility of paper with the dimensional qualities of cloth. But it is also my underlying hope that it will inspire you to create with abandon and outside of structure, to trust that art will realize itself if you trust your instinct.

The paper-cloth pieces used to create the projects came into being in a completely random fashion. As I worked on them, supplies were brought out as I thought of them, with no rhyme or reason, only intuition and trust. That was the only way to do it completely serendipitously. I found through trial and error that almost ANY combination worked as long as there was sufficient complexity, and I kept working them, obscuring previous layers.

The projects outlined here are for a variety of skill levels and offer a stunning array of color and design options that make an emotional impact. Paper quilts have become a popular form of expression because of the range of possibilities available to the beginning and advanced artist. Small art quilts are more accessible to beginning artists and they provide an excellent canvas for trying new techniques. But paper-cloth serves as a unique, designer fabric for a host of other creative endeavors. There are very few limits with this mixed media. Once you've mastered creating the base materials, the canvas is yours to fill.

It pleases me to think that this book is not a path, but the starting point for your ideas. The journey is truly yours. I hope you will find ways to summon inspiration and then to study the way it flows uniquely through you. Also, understand that art should be ritualistic, not in the sense that it is static and unchanging, but in the sense that it is a practice. You have a lifetime to perfect the practice, and some days will be more challenging than others, but creativity and serendipity will improve with dedication.

contents

foundations

an inTRODUCTION to PAPer-cloTH

The law of serendipity dictates that we cannot go searching for inspiration; we must take another journey and inspiration will find us. As you will see, I did not purposefully set out to discover paper-cloth. I was seeking to overcome a creative challenge, and my course of experimentation led me to it. The discovery of things not sought is one of the primary pleasures of creating. The art studio, whether it's a cavernous space or a place at the kitchen table, is the perfect place to abandon ourselves in play and delight in the process. By becoming absorbed in the act of creating, we allow chance to transform our work into something we never imagined. As you learn the fundamentals of paper-cloth, allow yourself to remain present and detach from artistic outcomes.

Paper and cloth are related in content and structure, so it is only natural to combine them. Anything that can be done to paper, from staining to crackling, can be done to mixed-media paper-cloth, only without blending dyes or soaking fabric in chemicals. Once finished, a paper and cloth fusion has all the strength of fabric, with the easy workability of paper. It's suitable for stitched quilts and an endless variety of projects from pillows to purses. Additionally, by combining cloth with paper, the medium becomes more familiar and the techniques more accessible. For example, quilters and fiber artists can now manipulate cloth without heavy processing that requires specialized equipment, lots of trial and error, and more open work space than many artists possess.

Inside this chapter, you will find the formula for basic paper-cloth. The materials are fun, some even quite humble, but the result you achieve with them is unmistakably full of potential.

THE PAPER-CLOTH PHENOMENON

PAPER + CLOTH = INFINITE POSSIBILITIES

The very first time I created paper-cloth, I was designing a paper quilt, which at the time, was a new thought in the land of mixed media. To me, the hallmark of a quilt is the stitching, and therefore, my own paper quilt needed to have a lot of stitching—hand or machine—in order to qualify as a quilt. But, stitched paper by itself is too fragile and flat to be interesting. Moreover, the idea of a paper quilt constructed simply as a collage and assembled with glue did not capture the warmth necessary to such a project.

As I researched possible methods, I was taken by fellow artist Beryl Taylor's approach to gluing paper to cloth. Clearly, this would allow me to embellish and apply surface designs to the paper while providing a strong enough substrate for a hearty dose of traditional quilt stitchery. I used Beryl's method to create some beautiful papers, then started experimenting with ways to juice up the color for my own work.

TRIAL AND ERROR

After laying out a half-dozen sheets of muslin and layering them with glue, tissue paper, and fun papers, I began adventuring with color. I started spraying the still-wet surfaces with brightly colored inks, then sponging the color around. Success was spotty, but encouraging. I hypothesized that dry paper-cloth would provide a much better base for loading with color.

Once the initial sheets of paper-cloth had cured overnight, I created more. My forthcoming experiments would have me endeavoring to obscure the features in the base of the paper. After another night of curing, I started applying color in earnest. I sponged and wiped and sprayed until I got the color I wanted. There was more opportunity to have a range of color and opacity while working dry. After the coloring agents were dry, the real fun began.

I looked at these sheets as kitchen-sink canvases, and one by one, I pulled out boxes of art supplies, from art markers and chalks to rubber stamps and embossing powders. What I did to one, I did to the rest. I'd write big bold script across the face of each sheet with different colors of markers. Then I'd ink up some big foam stamps and stamp images on each sheet in varying colors and prints. Then came embossing. The more I worked the sheets, the more I liked them.

Eventually I ended up with really rich, super-saturated, and deeply interesting sheets of patterned paper-cloth. They were so gorgeous on their own, it was difficult to cut into them to use them. I still have small pieces of these first sheets, and I treasure each bit, storing all of my scraps for later use.

My first paper-cloth quilts were of tulips, which is an homage to my home, Holland, Michigan. Holland is home to an annual tulip festival that draws upward of 500,000 people. We have thousands upon thousands of tulips blooming here each May. The colors and designs are stunning, and the history of the tulip is quite rich and interesting.

Mixed-media paper-cloth quilt with stitching
12" W x 12" H (30.48 x 30.48 cm)

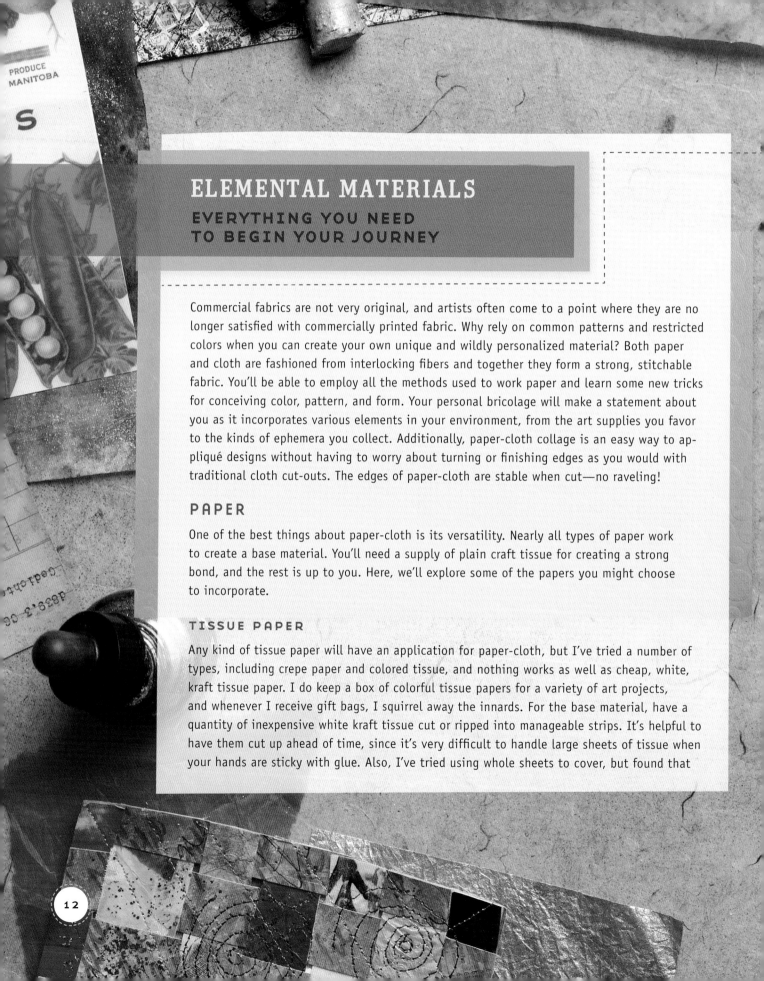

ELEMENTAL MATERIALS
EVERYTHING YOU NEED
TO BEGIN YOUR JOURNEY

Commercial fabrics are not very original, and artists often come to a point where they are no longer satisfied with commercially printed fabric. Why rely on common patterns and restricted colors when you can create your own unique and wildly personalized material? Both paper and cloth are fashioned from interlocking fibers and together they form a strong, stitchable fabric. You'll be able to employ all the methods used to work paper and learn some new tricks for conceiving color, pattern, and form. Your personal bricolage will make a statement about you as it incorporates various elements in your environment, from the art supplies you favor to the kinds of ephemera you collect. Additionally, paper-cloth collage is an easy way to appliqué designs without having to worry about turning or finishing edges as you would with traditional cloth cut-outs. The edges of paper-cloth are stable when cut—no raveling!

PAPER

One of the best things about paper-cloth is its versatility. Nearly all types of paper work to create a base material. You'll need a supply of plain craft tissue for creating a strong bond, and the rest is up to you. Here, we'll explore some of the papers you might choose to incorporate.

TISSUE PAPER

Any kind of tissue paper will have an application for paper-cloth, but I've tried a number of types, including crepe paper and colored tissue, and nothing works as well as cheap, white, kraft tissue paper. I do keep a box of colorful tissue papers for a variety of art projects, and whenever I receive gift bags, I squirrel away the innards. For the base material, have a quantity of inexpensive white kraft tissue cut or ripped into manageable strips. It's helpful to have them cut up ahead of time, since it's very difficult to handle large sheets of tissue when your hands are sticky with glue. Also, I've tried using whole sheets to cover, but found that it's better to have strips that crisscross. That allows for better adhesion of paper to fabric. Other tissue-type papers include napkins. Be on the lookout for these and save them if they have a nice color or pattern. Many artist's tissue papers are available and particularly lovely are those with a metallic design. When collaged over other images they impart a gilded feel and provide a sense of depth.

FUN PAPERS

Fun papers include anything and everything you have on hand, including wrapping paper, scrapbook papers, handmade papers, leftover pieces from other projects, dyed paper towels, origami papers, etc. Keep a scrap box and tuck in every little bit of paper littering your work space. I have a hard time letting these lovelies go, and they are perfect for the unrestrained abandon of paper-cloth. Even those papers you don't particularly love can add a delightful subtext when used in the initial layer of material. They will be covered by subsequent color and patterns and may be unrecognizable in final form.

RECYCLED PAPERS

Miscellany to recycle includes junk mail, food labels, magazine pages, book pages, candy wrappers, old sheet music, unwanted maps, newspapers, and crossword puzzles. Start collecting interesting specimens—ask people to send you brochures and newsletters in foreign languages. Also, sewing patterns, tea bags, coffee filters, and clothing hang tags are perfect pieces to experiment with. Look for almanacs, textbooks, large-print books, child's spellers, phone books, and atlases.

EPHEMERA

Ephemera is defined as transient everyday items meant to be thrown away. I love to use it in all of my artwork. Think about the small scraps of paper that slip through your fingers each day: Ticket stubs, grocery lists, notes, receipts, cards, letters, found items, postage stamps, and memorabilia. These paper gypsies move through the world and end up in the landfill, but they speak volumes about what occupies our daily lives. Capture these fleeting poems and embed them in your art.

CLOTH

Cloth forms a sturdy base and makes paper-cloth workable for sewn projects and quilts. Almost any woven material is a suitable substrate for paper layers, but opt for cotton when possible. As you work, parts of the base material may show through the finished work, so keep that in mind if you are considering using a preprinted or colored material. The only cautions to consider when choosing cloth are to avoid very thick or textured varieties and stretch synthetics. Bumpy surfaces may keep the paper from adhering, and cloth that is too thick, such as some interfacings, may take too long to dry. Choose fabrics without any stretch, as stretchy, synthetic materials will cause the paper layer to tear.

COTTON AND MUSLIN

Cotton, particularly unbleached muslin, forms the perfect foundation for paper-cloth. It's not necessary to choose finely woven muslin, as the addition of paper and glue will provide adequate strength for most projects. Cheaper muslins feature an open weave that adheres well to subsequent layers, so consider buying a bolt when you find a good sale. For the most part, it will be hidden by tissue, but if you want to show off a fabric design, leave open spaces when you are building up paper and tissue and your original fabric will shine through.

CANVAS

Canvas is the best choice for projects that require great strength. Choose unprimed cloth and look for less expensive options. Canvas is made of heavier fibers, enhancing it with great flexibility. But it's not necessary to choose a densely woven fabric, as paper and glue will form a better bond with a looser weave.

INTERFACING

Interfacing is a woven or nonwoven material for stabilizing sewing projects. Most interfacing will make a suitable base for paper-cloth, as long as it's not too thick. Thicker stabilizers cannot cure well enough and remain damp for an extended period. Interfacing remains pliable, so it's ideal for projects involving a lot of reworking. Experiment with a variety of interfacings to see which you like. Depending on the synthetic content of the interfacing, you may encounter separation of layers where the glue doesn't want to stick. Use additional glue or stitching to anchor the paper to the base. Avoid fusible materials—these are precoated with glue, which can become unstable and permanently sticky.

SHEER FABRICS

The use of sheer fabrics, such as organza, chiffon, tulle, and netting, result in a delightfully gossamer paper-cloth that can be used in the same way as muslin-based material, or it can be layered for effect. When applying paper and tissue to these fabrics, leave open areas and focus on a light covering with tissue paper and less opaque papers. If you have difficulty with the separation of layers because the base material cannot absorb glue, use stitching to anchor paper and fabric layers.

SUPPLIES

There are just a few more basic supplies required to begin making paper-cloth. Once you've created the base material, the rest of the process is fully adjustable to whatever art-making materials you have on hand.

GLUE

These projects and the creation of paper-cloth utilize basic white glue diluted with water in a 1:2 ratio—that is, one part glue to two parts water. You can find an assortment of white craft glues at most hobby supply stores. I prefer Aleene's Tacky Glue. If you're going to make a lot of paper-cloth, and I hope you do, look for quart- or gallon-size jugs of glue. Mix your diluted glue in a bucket with a lid and then close it between sessions. When you come back to it, add more water if necessary.

BRUSHES

You'll need some larger brushes for slathering on the glue. Either a 1½" (3.8 cm) bristle brush or a collection of foam brushes will suffice. The least expensive brushes are often the best, but choose one that will allow you to use pressure to press the paper into the fabric without tearing it. Plan to dedicate them to this process since they'll be coated in glue. I store my brush in the bucket of glue so it doesn't dry out and become stiff. If you're not going to be making paper-cloth for a while, clean off your brushes with warm, soapy water and vigorous rinsing.

FREEZER PAPER

Freezer paper makes an ideal base for not only this project but many other messy jobs. Try your local restaurant supply for an extra-large roll that will last a long time. Cut sheets to a manageable length and trim fabric to fit inside the dimensions of the freezer paper, allowing a good inch or so around all sides to collect excess glue. You will be working the paper-cloth all the way to the edges, so a border of freezer paper will protect your work surface. Use the glossy waxed side of the paper and your finished sheets will peel away from them easily. I reuse these sheets for later phases, when I'm coloring and stamping the fabric, so there is no need to throw them away.

WEAVING WONDERMENT
MIXING THE MAGIC THAT WILL BECOME PAPER-CLOTH

The first step in creating your paper-cloth is setting the stage. After you mix up a batch of paper-cloth, you can apply your own techniques to make the surface sing. The process is simple, but it's necessary to complete it and also to allow the resulting material to adequately dry before continuing. Plan to construct the base paper-cloth at least a day ahead of time. For me, it's most convenient to make a large batch of paper-cloth sheets that I can color and embellish later, when the mood strikes or the need arises. Once you begin working with paper-cloth, you'll find myriad uses in all of your mixed-media inspirations.

PREPPING THE SHEETS

To make one sheet of paper-cloth, cut a piece of base material, such as muslin, about 18" (45.7cm) long or as large as you want to work. Cut a piece of freezer paper slightly larger than the fabric base and lay the cloth on top of it, with the waxy side of the freezer paper facing up. If the cloth is wider than the freezer paper, use two overlapped sheets under the cloth. This will serve as a base as the paper-cloth dries, so you'll need a separate piece of freezer paper for each sheet of paper-cloth you make.

Cut or rip plain tissue paper into strips about 2" (5 cm) wide. This is just a suggestion. You may find that you prefer to use larger sheets of tissue paper as you work. Gather the other papers or ephemera and rip or cut them into workable strips or pieces.

I like to work with narrow sheets of tissue paper, but you should experiment to find what works for you.

MIXING THE GLUE

A small recycled bucket with a lid is a perfect receptacle for mixed glue. Use something you can dedicate to this purpose. An approximate glue-to-water ratio is 1:2. It's not necessary to be too picky about the glue dilution—find a consistency that works for you. The glue should be watered down enough to spread easily with a brush and to saturate all layers of the paper and cloth. This mixture will last a long time if covered between uses.

As you work, some of the tissue papers or other layers may bleed, especially if you are using previously painted or inked paper towels, newspapers, etc. It's best not to allow the glue to be stained by any errant pigment, so if you see this happening, wipe your brush off before dipping it back into the bucket.

BASIC CONSTRUCTION

Begin by saturating the base fabric with glue. Start in the middle and pull your brush toward the outside edges. As the glue wets the fabric, it will begin to stick to the freezer paper and become more stable. Brush the entire piece so that every part is coated with glue. If there are

any wrinkles, you can smooth them out with your fingers or the brush to create a nice flat piece of fabric, which will be beneficial for later stamping or journaling. Otherwise, if you want to experiment with textured paper-cloth, allow the wrinkles to remain.

Next, start layering strips of tissue and paper over the cloth, overlapping and changing direction until the entire sheet of cloth is mostly covered. It's okay to leave some fabric peeking through. As you lay each strip down, apply more diluted glue with the brush and tamp it down to adhere it to the fabric and the previous layers. Use a patting motion, rather than a sweeping motion with the brush. Keep a jar of water handy for cleaning off your brush so that you don't contaminate the glue bucket with unwanted color.

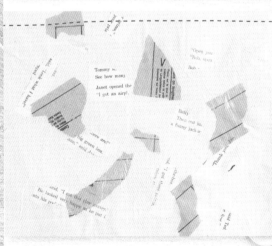

When applying glue, make sure to apply an even coat.

If you're having difficulty spreading glue that may have gotten too thick, or you waited too long to add paper and the surface has become tacky, simply spritz it with water. Additionally, some elements that are thinner and more gossamer, including tissue paper, may resist laying down nicely on the previous layer. If you float them down onto the surface, then spray them with a light wash of water, they will settle down enough that you can apply glue with the brush without disturbing them. Spray them and allow the water to soften them, then tamp them with the brush to adhere them to the paper-cloth. These steps form the foundation for paper-cloth.

TEXTURE

Paper-cloth naturally retains an interesting texture when you layer papers of varying weights and thicknesses. You can add more texture by deliberately crinkling up tissue paper as you work. Rather than trying to smooth out the tissue paper, let it form creases. These will add a lot of visual interest to the finished sheet, although it makes it more difficult to paint or journal. Try using some textured wallpapers or embossed papers collaged on to the surface. There will be opportunities to create texture at a later stage, but texture in this elementary material will interact with colors and embellishments as you work forward, so experiment with it.

These pieces of paper and ephemera will add a hint of depth, texture, and visual interest to the finished piece of paper-cloth.

Consider adding texture during the early stages of creating paper-cloth.

eMbrace Happy acciDents
turning mistakes into miracles

To err is human. Even seasoned artists fall into the trap of seeing their imperfections as failures. Have the courage to fail—mistakes add the soul to synchronicity and the innovation to imagination.

DISCOVER Exploration doesn't require a ship and a crew. You can discover new things by changing your perspective.

* Inject the familiar into each new art form. If you're a painter challenged by a quilt, try adding handpainted details. If you're a quilter challenged by a painting, try adding stitching. What you'll discover is something unique to you.

* Sometimes up is down and down is up. If your piece seems off, rotate or flip it, and view it with a new eye. You may find that you love the pattern that emerges when you let go of the status quo.

* "Failed" projects are excellent springboards. Keep a stash of projects you're not happy with, then cut them up, disassemble them, or use them as backgrounds for new works.

DETOUR When happenstance knocks you off the road, look for a trail, and enjoy the detour instead.

* Dealing with the unexpected requires flexibility. Take time to regroup, then begin again from where you've landed without looking back. When your project crosses to the dark side, decide that this is your funky piece and go wild.

* Fluid goals lead to concrete examples. You're more likely to be successful if you allow lots of mental wiggle room. If your planned oranges look more like apples, make a pie!

* Dead ends are only temporary. Let failures percolate, then come back to them at a later time, when you're more likely to see side roads. The quilt that didn't quite turn out might make some great fabric postcards.

EXPERIMENT It's difficult to be brave when the territory is uncharted. But serendipity happens when we are looking for something else. The key to progress is trying a variety of solutions.

* Employing "what if" scenarios is a great motivator. Should you accidentally leave something out, what would happen if you reversed steps or altered materials? If no one has ever done it before, all the better.

* Focus on the unexpected. If you accidentally dip your yellow brush in blue, start a love affair with green.

* Learning what doesn't work is valuable. Pop abject failures into a notebook and chalk them up as great experiences. There will be less of them than you think.

Snippets of text in a random pattern create an interesting base for paper-cloth.

EFFECTS

Many effects can be achieved at this stage as well.

- Cut lines of text out of a book, hold them over the wet paper-cloth and snip small squares with scissors, allowing the words and letters to fall to the surface in a random pattern. Tamp them with a glue brush to attach.

- Rip or cut small pieces of interesting, colorful fabrics and sprinkle them on the paper-cloth, then saturate them with glue to adhere them well.

- Add pieces of art fiber or yarn by laying down lengths on the wet paper-cloth and tamping them well with additional glue. As the paper-cloth dries, the fibers will become part of the base material.

Keep your fabric scraps handy when creating paper-cloth.

Art fibers and yarn can be incorporated into paper-cloth.

COLORING

Color as you work or see the next chapter for coloring options when dry. There are many ways to color paper-cloth. One is to add color during the gluing stage. One of the benefits of this is the tendency of the color to penetrate different papers and the cloth with varying levels of intensity. Try spritzing the surface with diluted ink or acrylic paint and working it into the background with the brush. Don't forget to rinse the brush in water before putting it back in the glue. If you decide not to add color at this point, don't worry. There will be many more ways to infuse your paper-cloth with saturated color in the next section.

FINISHING

Leave the paper-cloth sheets on freezer paper and set them somewhere to dry overnight or for at least a few hours. Here's a simple drying system to speed up curing time. Hang a clothesline in your work area and use clothespins to hang the paper-cloth until dry. Be sure to put down some newspaper to catch glue drips. The paper-cloth may curl up a bit as it dries, but you can iron it later. After the paper-cloth is dry, remove it from the freezer paper by placing it face down and slowly peeling the freezer paper away. Keep the freezer paper to use as a working surface for coloring and marking your sheets. Iron the paper-cloth sheet to flatten it. This is the best time to do this, since some of the surface treatments may render it unsuitable for ironing later. Use a hot iron without steam and cover the paper-cloth with a nonstick ironing sheet to keep from getting glue on your iron. Iron both sides and store the sheet flat for best results.

Once you've created some fabulous paper-cloth sheets that incorporate paper, tissue, and other elements, such as ephemera and text, get ready to explore a range of surface treatments that will make your material sizzle. You may choose to add just a few techniques, or continue experimenting until every square inch is artfully appropriated. This process naturally contains a modicum of chaos, so don't think too hard as you move forward. Just create and enjoy the results, and if things don't turn out as you've expected, add another wash of color, a mask of gesso, or a bit of collage. If that doesn't work, get out the sandpaper and scrub away until you're satisfied. The only science is play.

Coloring paper-cloth at its base will allow the color to saturate each layer, adding richness.

serendipity
discover the joy of creating paper-cloth

Serendipity Collage means you let go of structure and venture into new territory. It means creating in a random pattern and abandoning the idea of "designing" the end result; contrived work will be apparent. Get ready to leave common fabrics and commercial predictability behind and work with an open mind to deliver a truly complex piece of cloth.

There is an element of chaos that feels intimidating but at the same time reassuring because there are no disasters, no accidents, and no failures. Paper-cloth is about layers of creativity. Each new mark you make will build on everything that came before. Let your intuition guide you as you go. Start with one or two processes, then continue to add more until you believe the work is done. Trust yourself. Have fun. Play and learn.

I don't believe that talent is a tangible gift bestowed on some people and not on others. From my perspective, chance favors those who are prepared with an arsenal of techniques and practiced abilities. The following section is a workbook designed to spark ideas that you will try for yourself. More than eighty examples of paper-cloth are introduced, each one accompanied by an explanation of materials and techniques. This is a great starting point should you need a friendly push in the right direction. Plus, there are a few activities aimed at challenging you to exercise your creative muscle. As you journey further into serendipity, nothing is a waste of time—each intimate act of creation plants a seed.

INVITING JUICINESS
SATURATE YOUR PAPER-CLOTH WITH JUICY COLOR

If paper-cloth is juicy, it is infused with so much color and boldness that it can't hold any more. Sure, you can use paper-cloth in its organic state, but even if you've created an interesting piece with lots of visual play, color is the key to transforming it into a serendipitously delightful material. Inks, paints, powders, and stains are your ingredients, and this is your recipe book.

COLORING WITH INKS AND STAINS

Inks are probably my very favorite coloring medium. They come in a wide range of types, including permanent, pigment, dye-based, pearlescent, metallic, and india inks. All of them can be diluted if necessary, and most can be mixed for special colors. They can be applied with sponges, brushes, pens, or splattered and dripped. Wear gloves when working with inks, as they can easily stain your hands or creep under your fingernails, where you can't reach them.

Water-soluble inks, like Adirondack Color Wash, are water-resistant when dry, but blend with water when wet. Some calligraphy and drawing inks are also soluble dye. Waterproof inks include bright acrylics and pearlescent formulas. India ink is highly pigmented, leaving a brilliant, transparent finish. Other inks have a fuller pigment base, making them more opaque. Re-inkers are also fun to use and generally contain intense, concentrated ink. Look at the bottle to see what kind of properties your ink has.

ACRYLIC INK

Pour some acrylic ink into a small spray bottle and add a little water. Spritz the paper-cloth until you achieve the color saturation you want. Drip or splatter drops of other ink colors while it's still wet.

to create this piece: Spritz orange acrylic ink, then dribble red ink while still wet. Stamp squares with orange acrylic paint applied to a foam stamp. Stitch with contrasting thread.

INDIA INKS

India inks are highly saturated and very permanent. Take care if applying them over paper or features you don't want to completely cover. Invest in inexpensive eyedroppers so that you don't mix colors.

to create this piece: Collage some book text and illustrations to paper-cloth. Hold vertically and drip ink, allowing it to run onto a piece of newspaper.

SPRAYING

Inks will display different properties when sprayed. Some will even out as if washed with a brush, and others will leave discrete droplets. If you like the mottled look of a sprayed pattern, first spray the whole sheet of paper-cloth with a single color of water-based ink. Use a paper towel to wipe off the excess and rub the color into any lighter areas. Then respray, this time allowing the ink to dry on its own. Keep your stained wiping towels for use in paper collage.

to create this piece: Spray with butterscotch-colored soluble ink and wipe with a paper towel. Lightly spray with butterscotch, espresso, and plum ink and allow to dry undisturbed. Use an awl to punch holes and add eyelets, then string wire and add a shipping tag.

BLOTTING

The interaction of ink on ink is determined by both the types of ink and also the surface you're applying it to. When you create a color wash with ink, then drop more ink on top, it will dilute the original layer, allowing some of it to be removed and creating a new color where the first layer has stained the surface.

to create this piece: Collage colorful hand-printed papers on top of the paper-cloth. Spray with green color wash, then drip butterscotch ink on top and quickly blot it up. Apply a fancy machine stitch in green thread.

25

DRIPPING

Each type of ink has a drip footprint. Keep a spritz bottle of water handy for helping it along as it meanders down the page. Lay down some heavy paper towels, or even better, some freezer paper, to catch drips.

to create this piece: Hold the paper-cloth sheet vertically and squirt drops of pink waterproof-dye ink along the top. Spray drips with water as they begin to run, to aid in their movement. Add more ink and spritz again, then drop yellow inks and let them run as well. When they have all run off the page, allow it to dry, then mimic the drips with a free-motion stitch in pink thread.

DIRECT STAMP PAD

You can apply the ink from a stamp pad directly to surfaces by pouncing or dragging it across the surface of paper-cloth to apply color. Except for those containing permanent or solvent-based ink, most ink pads are slow drying, so don't mix two colors or you'll muddy the pads. Permanent-ink pads, like Staz-On, give a harder, more differentiated look. Chalk and pigment pads are softer and will fill in valleys with color.

to create this piece: Press a light-toast-colored chalk stamp pad over the surface and rub it around to cover. Lightly brush a purple stamp pad over the top, skimming the surface. Use fabric glue to adhere an illustration printed on glossy photo paper. Spray the photo with water and scratch it with an awl. Color with alcohol inks and stitch with a free-motion machine stitch.

ALCOHOL INKS

Alcohol inks can be used on any nonporous surface from metals to glass, making them excellent partners for paper-cloth. They can be washed, dripped, mottled, or marbled. On hard surfaces, they are very forgiving, so mistakes can be removed with alcohol. A little goes a long way, as long as you work fast. They dry as quick as lightning. You can purchase dabbers and pads or cut your own pads from inexpensive felt. I've also applied them with a small paintbrush to buttons, photos, and other objects. Use rubbing alcohol to clean your brushes when you're finished.

to create the first piece (top): Drip on butterscotch alcohol ink and spread it over the surface with a small piece of felt. Drip terra-cotta alcohol ink in different areas and pounce with a blotter to blend. Splatter with a few extra drops of a darker color. Stitch around collaged areas with variegated thread in oranges and russets.

to create the second piece (bottom): Apply a range of green alcohol inks (lettuce, meadow, oregano) and pounce to blend. Stitch on a photo. Spritz with water and let it run over the photo, then blot it with a paper towel. Drip green and butterscotch alcohol ink and dab with blotter to blend.

WALNUT INK

Walnut ink creates a warm, nicely aged appeal. If you purchase crystals, you can mix up a range of colours, from lighter washes to dark stains. I keep mine in jam jars, premixed and ready to use. They are usually potent; test a small area for best results. Different textures and surfaces will react differently as they soak up the stain. One way to highlight these differences is to over collage some bits of paper to create a more porous area. Another way is to make sure you're leaving areas of fabric showing through on the base paper-cloth.

to create this piece: Apply a wide wash of diluted walnut ink and wipe with a paper towel. Dribble and spritz concentrated walnut ink and allow to dry naturally or blast with a heat gun. Draw circles with a bronze metallic paint pen. Stamp and emboss with distress powders and a barcode stamp. Machine stitch swirls with variegated thread and handstitch spirals with dyed cotton floss.

COFFEE AND TEA STAINING

Coffee and tea stain differently than other inks and stains, resulting in a range of tints from tan to muddy brown. You can let chance take its course by leaving damp tea bags and leaves or coffee crystals and grounds on the paper-cloth. Spritz the surface with water to help them along, then brush them off when dry to reveal the pattern.

to create this piece: Apply a wash of walnut ink infused with coffee and allow it to stain. Sprinkle coffee crystals while the surface is wet and allow to dry. Rub off the excess with a paper towel. Stamp with a foam stamp and black acrylic paint. Stitch around collaged elements with gold thread and stamp dots with gold paint.

COLORING WITH PAINTS AND GLAZES

Paint is the quintessential art medium. It's the life blood of art supplies. Each has its own properties. Acrylic paint is versatile and offers advantages across a broad spectrum. Water-color paints are delicate but can bleed if they get wet during a later technique. Oil-based paints and glazes are also available. The next few pages will cover these materials as well as a variety of techniques to try when using them.

ACRYLIC PAINT

There are many different ways to apply acrylic paint, and each technique will require a specific consistency. Acrylic paints are colorfast, permanent, and wonderfully flexible. Their vibrancy is not diluted when watered down, and they are fast drying, which gives them a versatility not found in other paint mediums. Their durability is a plus when creating stitched projects that will get a lot of wear and tear. Heavy-bodied paints are great for stamping and are more opaque when working on paper-cloth. Fluid acrylics are perfect for painting on, glazing, and washing large areas. You can also pour them into spray bottles and add water for a readymade color spray. Once they're dry, other colors can be added over them without mixing colors.

to create this piece: Wash the surface with diluted glue and sprinkle on squares of cut book text. Quilt stitch free-motion style with orange thread. Spray with a diluted acrylic wash of orange. Rip bits of painted newspaper and collage to the paper-cloth. Stamp with stars in orange and yellow acrylic paint.

WHITE PAINT PENS

Marks made with white paint have a very different feel than black. They make objects pop off the page and glow. Use white paint pens to highlight images, doodle, or journal. Each manufacturer has a different formula, so try a variety and choose the one you like best, then stock up.

to create this piece: Brush on pink glaze, then coat with interference paint. Stamp the surface with white acrylic paint and a rubber stamp. Use gel medium to adhere a translucent liquid clay transfer. Cut out eggs from paper-cloth and glue them on. Stitch around the entire image, using a free-motion stitch. Mark around the image elements with a white paint pen.

29

PULLING

There are different ways to achieve patterns in paint. Pulling is a quick and fun method that adds a lot of texture. Lay down a coat of acrylic paint on the paper-cloth, then place a piece of paper face down on the surface. Press it with your hand to make full contact with the paint. Pull the paper off, taking some of the paint with it and leaving a pattern. Reverse this process and paint the paper, then press the paper-cloth onto the surface and pull it away for a sparser design. Try pressing two sheets of paper-cloth together to color both at the same time.

to create this piece: Use a brush to apply a layer of blue acrylic paint. Place a piece of freezer paper on top and press it into the paint, then pull the freezer paper off. Blot some paint off with a paper towel and allow to dry thoroughly. Collage on some circles cut from book pages and draw around them with oil pastels. Stitch stems by machine, using a zigzag stitch.

SPLATTERING

Things get wild in my studio, which is why I try to make sure that any finished artwork is moved to a different area. Splattering is a fun way to infuse a large area with color, pattern, or texture. Splatter light colors on dark, dark colors on light, contrasting colors on each other, and white, black, or metallics on everything. A paintbrush serves well much of the time, but try a hair comb and a toothbrush to see how the patterns differ. To use a paintbrush, dip it in water first, then paint. Flick it toward the paper by snapping your wrist. You'll end up with large and small drips and some that fan out in a row. To use a toothbrush, dip the bristles in paint, then pull the head of the brush over a palette knife or the handle of a paintbrush. This will create a more uniform pattern of small dots and splatters.

to create this piece: Apply a wash of plum and butterscotch inks and allow to dry. Stamp diamonds with a rubber stamp and black permanent-ink pad. Splatter metallic gold paint with the tip of a paintbrush, changing direction as you go. Free-motion stitch flowers with metallic threads.

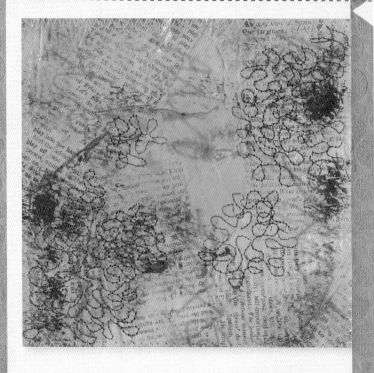

SPONGING

Some sponges have neatly arranged holes, and some are a crazy network of recesses. Unless you've cut a shape from a sponge and are trying to stamp a pattern, you don't want defined edges. With a sea sponge's round shape, you don't really have to worry about that. If you're using a square sponge, either flex it in your hand so that the edges don't appear or just apply paint to the center and avoid the hard edges. Be sure to wash out the sponge or pop it into your rinse water—dried paint will ruin it. You can sponge with non-traditional things like a wad of newsprint or a paper towel—the effect is similar. To sponge on color, allow the first coat of paint to dry, then sponge on a lighter or darker color. Don't load up the sponge with too much color—you can dab it on a piece of paper first to prepare it. To remove color, brush on a coat of paint and apply the sponge while the first coat is still wet. You can incorporate tiny amounts of a new color and blend them in.

to create this piece: Apply a coat of yellow acrylic ink. Write with a dark yellow marker. Lightly sponge on nickel azo color with a sea sponge. Free-motion quilt with russet thread.

SCRAPING

It's almost a shame to dilute those scrumptious paints right out of the tube. All their saturated glory is intensified when they're applied thickly. Scraping adds texture and preserves the full beauty of the pigment.

to create this piece: Apply a few dabs of red and white heavy body acrylic along two sides of the paper-cloth. With a rubber scraper, palette knife, or credit card, pull the paint across the page. Draw in the other direction to mix the rest. Give the thick paint time to dry, then zigzag stitch with pink thread.

31

COMBING

Combing is an easy way to create lines on your paper-cloth. You can use a paint comb or a hair comb. Each offers a unique pattern. Practice combing designs on paper, doing straight lines, waves, and loops until you are happy with your results. If it doesn't turn out the way you'd hoped, smooth out the paint and try again.

to create this piece: Paint the background with orange paint. Apply a thick, even layer of yellow textile paint with a brayer or brush. Use a paint comb to draw waves over the surface and allow to dry well. Stitch with a zigzag of yellow thread.

WATERCOLORS

I've always loved the look of watercolors but often failed to achieve the look I wanted until I discovered artist's quality tube paints. Quality makes a huge difference in color saturation. Because paper-cloth is somewhat nonporous, it doesn't take water-based paints well. But watercolor paints out of the tube look marvelous, retaining their translucent feel while adding intense color. If the color is too much, spritz with water and blot some of it off. Try mixing colors by brushing a second color in and working the brush to mix the two.

to create this piece: Collage on vintage text and images. Apply tube watercolor in orange and pink with a stiff bristle brush. Lightly spritz areas with water and blot with a paper towel to highlight. Stitch by machine with a free-motion bubble pattern and pink thread.

GLAZES

There are glazing mediums available that will allow the paint to float on the surface and slow down the drying process. These are added to acrylic paints to dilute them. You can also purchase colored glaze that has already been premixed. I prefer to mix my own so that I can control the opacity and retain saturated color. Glazes are easy to use. It's just a matter of brushing them on and waiting for them to dry. If you find that you want a more opaque look, add more paint and recoat.

to create this piece: Add purple acrylic paint and iridescent pearl paint to a small amount of acrylic glazing medium. Use a brush to apply the resulting mixture to paper-cloth.

OIL STICKS

Paint sticks or oil sticks are similar to oil pastels but give the look and feel of real oil paint. Like pastels, they will need a few days to cure but then become light-fast and permanent. Use them to highlight or finish edges, as well as to cover large areas. Once you've applied the oil crayon, use your fingers to smooth it out and give it a soft appearance. My favorites of this group are the metallics. They add a nice bit of sparkle to many mixed-media projects and come in a number of rich colors.

to create this piece: Scribble on a purple paint stick and use your fingers and a cloth to rub it into the surface. Allow it to cure for a few days, then free-motion machine stitch with metallic purple thread.

BRAYERING

You can brayer paint directly on surfaces, creating multiple patterns. Depending on how hard you press, it will either ride on the top of textured surfaces or fill in the entire area. You can treat them like paint rollers—squeeze out some acrylic paint on a palette and run the roller through it to coat it, then apply the paint to the surface by rolling the brayer back and forth, changing directions until the paint is gone. Try squeezing paint directly on the roller or applying small dots of paint to the surface, then rolling the brayer back and forth to move the paint around.

to create this piece: Apply random dots of blue and green paint to the surface and spread with a brayer. Add more dots of paint if desired and repeat. Print an image on an ink-jet transparency and cut it out. Apply gel medium to the back of a piece of dyed fabric and adhere the transparency. Use fabric glue to adhere to the background, then stencil pink paint alphabet letters.

RAGGING

With ragging you can achieve a softer effect than with sponging. Paper towels work well if you don't want to commit to using an actual rag. Get the cloth or paper towel well coated with paint and scrunch it up a few times during the process to change the patterns. The more you pounce the rag, the softer the final effect will be.

to create this piece: Place a dollop of purple, pink, and interference paint on a palette. Wad up a paper towel or rag and dip it in all three colors. Begin dabbing it on the paper-cloth in a sponging motion until all areas are covered and blended.

METALLICS

Nothing adds sparkle and shine like metallics. Look for them in powder form, in paint, in tubes and in pens. They are a nice way to finish and to highlight borders or elements.

METAL POWDERS

These beautiful shimmers stick to water and wet media and can be used in several ways. You can sprinkle them directly into your paint or ink or dust them over the wet media, where they'll adhere when dried. They are a much more intense metallic effect than other powdered mediums. TroCol powder comes in golds, bronzes, and silver. The silver is not as fine as the gold but has its own charm.

to create this piece: Wash with metallic gold glaze and, while wet, lightly sprinkle with pale gold TroCol powder. Allow to dry and machine stitch triangles with metallic thread.

METALLIC FABRIC PAINT

Fabric paints naturally lend themselves to paper-cloth, and there is an amazing selection of colors. Some fabric paints may not be as saturated as acrylics, but they'll have a more glazed appearance because of the binders. Lumiere metallic acrylics can be used for fabric and crossover well to other mixed media, producing gorgeous results. They are intensely metallic and nicely opaque, with a deep richness.

to create this piece: Wash background with bronze metallic textile paint, wiping away some areas. With a paintbrush, splatter purple acrylic paint over the surface. Create a paper flower by gluing layers of ripped specialty paper strips to make petals. Edge the petals with gold paint pen and use clear embellishment glue to adhere pearls or beads.

INTERFERENCE PAINT

Also known as opalescents, interference paints are colorless glazes with the addition of mica flakes. The mica reflects light to create colors that seem to float on the surface. You can mix them with other paints to impart the shimmer or over glaze an entire area to add shine. A number of manufacturers make interference paints that shimmer in an iridescent glow. Some of them have very fine glitter as well.

to create this piece: Brush on a coat of iridescent, glittery interference paint. Stitch a heart of paper-cloth over a square of paper-cloth and embellish it with collaged text. Apply a small piece of fusible web to one side of the heart and iron on fabric foil. Adhere a small piece of fusible web to another side of the heart and iron on angelina fibers. Use clear-drying glue to add small beads and free-motion stitch designs in coordinating thread.

METALLIC WAX PASTE

Rub 'N Buff is a metallic wax paste that is available in many colors. Use it wherever there is a textured surface to highlight. Squeeze a little out of the tube onto a palette and mix in any of the oil that has separated. Rub some on the pad of your finger and then lightly brush it across the surface, making contact with the high points. The wax leaves an impervious golden shimmer that is permanent. It's less shiny than gold leaf or a gold pen, but it imparts a deeper, more matte-like finish.

to create this piece: Adhere crumpled up tissue paper with diluted glue. Drip waterproof dye ink on the surface and use a felt pad to spread it around to cover. Lightly touch the high points with Rub 'N Buff, using your fingertips. Stitch designs with gold metallic thread.

SHIMMER SPRAY

Shimmer sprays look divine on paper-cloth projects. They are available in multiple colors with an ultra-fine mica additive. You can make your own by adding some TroCol powder to a spray bottle of diluted ink or try Radiant Rain misters. Radiant Rain contains both color and shimmer that adds a subtle shine to paper and mixed media.

to create this piece: Spritz persimmon shimmer spray to color. Apply purple oil paint stick to the bottom of a cardboard tube, rub it in, and then use it to stamp circles. Soften the stamped lines with your finger. Machine stitch purple circles.

METAL LEAF

Gold leaf, plus its silver, bronze, and red cousins, makes a beautiful statement. These super thin sheets of metal will stick to anything slightly tacky, so make sure your hands are clean before picking one up. For best results, brush on special metal-leaf adhesive and allow it to dry until it's tacky. Lay a sheet of metal leaf over the adhesive and brush it with a paintbrush to remove the excess leaf. Save the extra bits for another project.

to create this piece: Color the background with plum, purple, and butterscotch alcohol inks, dripping and blotting. Brush gold-leaf adhesive randomly over the surface and allow it to dry until tacky. Lay down pieces of assorted color metallic leaf, press, and brush with a dry paintbrush. Stitch lines with gold thread.

METALLIC OIL STICKS

Metallic oil sticks write on most surfaces. Shiva Paint Sticks come in beautiful metallic colors like green, blue, red, orange, and pink. Remove the dried coating by rubbing it on a piece of scrap paper or twisting it with a paper towel. Let the finished paper-cloth cure for a few days to set the paint and make it permanent.

to create this piece: Spray with lettuce water-based ink and dab with green alcohol inks. Draw a grid with a green metallic oil-paint stick and soften it with your finger. Highlight some of the squares by stitching with gold metallic thread.

METALLIC GLUE-GUN ACCENTS

Glue guns aren't just for gluing two parts together, they make an excellent surface design. Glue sticks even come in a range of colors, including gold. Heat the glue and use the gun to doodle on the surface. Once you've created a design on the paper-cloth, you can color it in multiple ways. Try smoothing on some Rub 'N Buff with your fingers or brush on alcohol inks for a transparent look. Create swirls, dots, borders, and more.

to create this piece: Spray on butter-scotch and lettuce color-wash ink, then stamp images with gold paint. Stamp numbers in black acrylic paint. Draw swirls and dots with a glue gun and allow to cool. Brush over the glue with gold-leaf pen.

CHALKS AND MARKERS

Serendipity brings a certain innocence to art. It doesn't matter what kind of look you seek; it's the fact that you are just sitting down to play creatively. When using chalks and art markers, I am even further transported to my safe haven of no judgment, just art. Chalks and markers can create looks both bold and soft.

ART MARKERS

Think of markers as ink in stick form. The ink is wicked out as you write. Most good-quality artist's markers will write on paper-cloth. If you're having trouble, use a permanent marker—they now come in a range of colors.

to create this piece: Wash the background with pearlescent acrylic ink in peach, then drip with darker ink. Take a blue artist's marker and write text at random across the page. Use matching blue thread to thread sketch (see pages 63 and 98 for more details) along the lines of the text.

CHALK PASTELS

Pastels are pigment in powdered form—they have a binder that just holds them together. They need something to adhere to, so the best way to use them on paper-cloth is either to coat it first with clear gesso (gesso provides tooth) or to lay down some other medium first. If the paper-cloth will be used in something that will be handled, spray it with a fixative to set the pastels and protect the surface.

to create this piece: Fill in the background color by applying a pink chalk pad directly to the surface. Rub pink pastel chalk over the design. Stitch with metallic thread.

REDUCING AND REMOVING COLOR

When you've added too much color or you want to prepare a background for text or illustration, consider washing the background with gesso. There are several effects to choose from, and they'll help prepare the surface for the next layer. Conversely, adding color and then removing it does not mean you've changed your mind. Sometimes that's the best way to find a new color—the one created by the process. Agents for removing color include bleach, water, alcohol, and sandpaper. Be prepared for interesting results. You can always add color back in if you've gone too far.

WHITE GESSO

Acrylic gesso is a polymer-medium primer that prepares a surface for receiving paint. White gesso contains a pigment that's markedly opaque. If you want to tone down the background of paper-cloth to prepare it for journaling or painting, you can brush on white gesso as a glaze. A full coat will completely cover and leave a chalky surface. Add paint to white gesso to tint it pastel. Clear gesso is useful for creating a ground that paint can adhere to, but use white for these projects.

to create this piece: Brush on a diluted coat of white gesso and immediately wipe some of it off with a paper towel. Sponge on more to cover some areas and leave the rest peeking through. Free-motion stitch with white thread.

WHITE UNDERCOAT

Use white gesso to mute the background, then coat it with shimmer spray or interference paints. Add subtle interest with pastel art markers or stamping and embossing in light shades. This will create a paper-cloth that is white-hued, but with a lot of character.

to create this piece: Wash the paper-cloth with a thin glaze of white gesso and coat with pearl paint. Write and doodle with pastel art markers. Stamp text and images with taupe and white acrylic paint. Dab with embossing fluid, sprinkle platinum ultra-thick embossing enamel and melt with a heat gun. Affix a paper-cloth heart and stitch.

BLOTTING OUT COLOR

I keep a couple of spray bottles in the studio. One is full of water and the other contains rubbing alcohol. Both work to remove color or help it move along. They react differently with various mediums, so play with them to find a look you like. Don't wait too long after applying color to try and remove it, or it may stain the surface and become permanent.

to create this piece: Rub the surface with purple acrylic paint on a paper towel, getting it into the crevices. Spritz with alcohol and use a clean paper towel to burnish and remove color. Spray with alcohol again and continue removing color to reveal the images below.

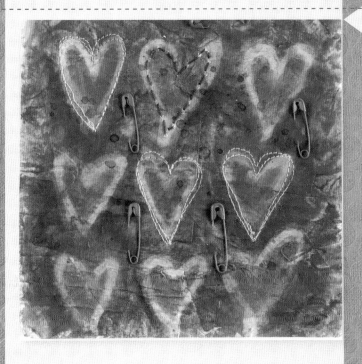

BLEACH PEN

You can find bleach gel pens at the grocery store. They have many uses, from fabric to altered photos. When you use them on fabric, it's best to wash the resulting cloth in a bleach stop agent to protect it from further deterioration. With paper-cloth you won't have the opportunity to do that, so just wipe it well to remove as much as possible. Shake the pen before you use it and squeeze a little bit out on scrap paper until you get to the gel. Write, doodle, or draw on a dyed or stained surface, wait a few moments (longer if necessary), then wipe the bleach off quickly with paper towel. Rub it with a clean paper towel.

to create this piece: Color the background with green ink, then wipe on some fabric paint. Draw hearts with a bleach gel pen, wait one minute, then wipe well with a clean paper towel. Emphasize the bleached area by filling in the hearts with more ink. Stitch around some of the hearts on the machine and hand embroider others with green floss. Attach rusted safety pins.

41

CASTING CHANCE
COMBINE CREATIVE TECHNIQUES TO PROVOKE SERENDIPITY

Creativity is simply a serendipitous chain of events leading to happy accidents. Can you create chance? You can certainly improve your own opportunities by utilizing a broad spectrum of techniques. Don't be afraid to apply more than one action to a sheet of paper-cloth. The cumulation of skills is the best way to cast your luck. Sift through books about using paint, paper, and fabric and appropriate anything and everything. Mixed media is not for the faint of heart. Stamp, stitch, and collage, then go back and emboss, print, alter, and bead.

SERENDIPITY SQUARES

I once taught a class on serendipity squares. I asked students to stamp, sponge, and collage on an old map. Each sheet was amazingly unique in color and composition, yet, when cut up and combined they worked. I've discovered that there is a "tipping point" when serendipity surfaces and seemingly random acts of art produce cohesive, versatile patterns that work with anything.

MOSAIC PIECES

Serendipity squares are perfect for creating mosaic squares. Adhere scraps to poster board (or card stock for less dimension). Spray glue is ideal, but gel medium will work. Apply glue to both the poster board and the paper-cloth and smooth them together. After they've dried, cut them into strips and then into squares. Coat your final piece with thick varnish or ultra-thick embossing enamel, and it will look just like ceramic and glass.

to create this piece: Dab on red alcohol ink to cover, then drip lighter colors and blot up. Use gel medium to adhere pieces of paper-cloth to black poster board or card stock. With a paper cutter, cut 1" (2.54 cm) squares, then, if desired, cut those into quarters. Run a gold leaf pen around the outside of each square and affix to paper-cloth with fabric glue.

STAMPING

When stamping, there is no need to ink the whole thing or even stay on the page. Stamps are for play. You can use commercial stamps or make your own from foam. Use your stamps to create backgrounds, render text, or embellish wild surfaces.

BASIC STAMPING

The best way to ink a stamp is to tap it with the stamp pad or dab a paint-loaded cosmetic sponge directly on the stamp surface, rather than pouncing the stamp on the ink or directly in the paint. This will give you more control and avoid unwanted lines from the stamp edges. Place the item to be stamped on a slightly soft surface, such as a pad of paper, so that the stamp is able to make full contact, and you don't have to rock it (which could create a double image).

to create this piece: Drip light green ink and apply it with a paintbrush to cover. Rub an orange oil pastel over the surface. Use a foam stamp and stamp rectangles both in dark green and yellow. Machine stitch around the stamps with a straight and zigzag stitch and yellow thread.

OVERSTAMPING

Double stamping the same image with an overlap adds depth. Make a slight change in the color by lightening or darkening it for the second round of stamping.

to create this piece: Apply turquoise paint to the background. Use a sponge to load a foam stamp with blue paint and stamp repeatedly until the paint is gone. Add a little white to the blue and stamp again, slightly overlapping the first set of stamps. Stitch around the stamped image.

43

WHITE STAMPING

White accents rise to just about any art occasion. Like a hint of gold, a little bit of white adds an element of visual interest, lightens up the design, or it can create the illusion of negative space.

to create this piece: Collage on polka-dotted tissue paper. Color the background by brushing on red textile paint. Stitch circles with black thread. Apply strips of decorative fabric tape. Stencil white dots by using a cosmetic sponge to tamp white paint through a piece of sequin waste.

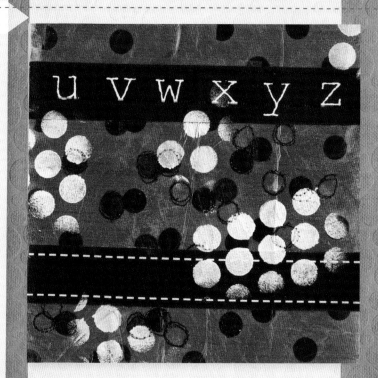

HANDMADE FOAM STAMPS

I have a lot of handmade craft-foam stamps because they're inexpensive to make and a little addictive. You'll want to find foam that's a little thicker than the average sheets, so look for other things made out of craft foam, such as books, hats, door hangers, etc. Use a piece of foam or blocks of acrylic for the base. Cut the foam into shapes with scissors and adhere them to the base with white glue. Wait for the stamp to dry completely before using it. They wash up nicely, but don't let them sit in the water for long.

to create this piece: Brush the background with orange india ink to stain. Apply green acrylic paint to a foam stamp and stamp it repeatedly until the paint is gone. Add zigzag stitching to accent.

HANDMADE SPONGE STAMPS

Craft stores sell compressed sponges that are flatter than a pancake, at least any pancake that I've ever seen. Cut them with scissors to make elementary shapes, such as a heart, for stamping. Don't try anything intricate because the detail will be lost when the sponge springs to life in water. Reconstitute the sponge when you're ready to use it and squeeze out all the excess water. Dip it in paint and stamp. The holes in the sponge will make a nice texture if it's not too heavily loaded with paint. Toss it in your rinse water when finished.

to create this piece: Embed colorful fibers in the paper cloth with a wash of diluted glue. Cut a heart out of a compressed sponge and rehydrate it with water. Use a brayer to roll out some pink acrylic paint, tamp the sponge in the paint, and stamp hearts. Stitch around them with contrasting thread and stamp numbers on the hearts with paint.

CARVED STAMPS

Carving your own stamps is a rewarding process, but it takes more time and is more costly than making foam or sponge stamps. You'll need a special soft block, a linoleum sheet, or you can use an eraser for smaller projects. There are cutting tools made especially for carving stamps, and they have a curved, V-shaped blade set in a handle. Draw your design on the carving sheet with a permanent marker or place a black photocopied image face down and rub the back with a cotton ball dipped in acetone, then burnish to transfer the image. Decide which areas you want in relief and carve those out of the block. If you want to carve a stamp with text, you'll need to reverse it first. Many artists leave some imperfections and hatch-mark lines so that it is apparent that the image was carved by hand.

to create this piece: For the background, splatter gold metallic paint. Add a coat of glitter paint. Load a hand-carved stamp with black paint and stamp it on a piece of yellow paper-cloth. Adhere the image with glue and stitch around it with black thread.

TEXTURIZING

Paper-cloth is not a dainty material—it is meant to be handled. Why not invite touch with texture? Texture can be applied to paper-cloth in its initial stages, or you can layer it on after you've created the base. Texture can be subtle or bold. It's important to understand your texturizing materials as, once dry, some are meant to be flexible while others will remain static. There are myriad ways to achieve texture and dozens of effects with which you can experiment.

SPRAY WEBBING

This fun spray shoots out a web of metallic filament that bonds to the surface. It looks best against a very dark or very light background. Try spraying it first and then painting over it to create a textured surface, or highlight it with a gold paint pen.

to create this piece: Apply purple acrylic ink with a paintbrush dipped in the bottle. Shake a can of gold spray webbing and hold it about 18" (45.7 cm) away from the background. Spray the webbing, moving back and forth to create a random pattern. When the webbing is dry, stitch around the images to accent them.

WAXED PAPER

Waxed paper has a lot of interesting properties. It's thin enough to see through, repels various paints and inks and creates a nice crackled feature when crumpled up. To get the crackled look, crumple it up well, then iron it back out.

to create this piece: Crumple up a piece of waxed paper, then iron it. Spray it with purple and butterscotch water-based ink and blot it dry. Place the waxed paper over the paper-cloth and stitch it in place with a free-motion stitch. Drip and blot more purple ink, then stamp stars with gold paint sponged on cookie cutters.

46

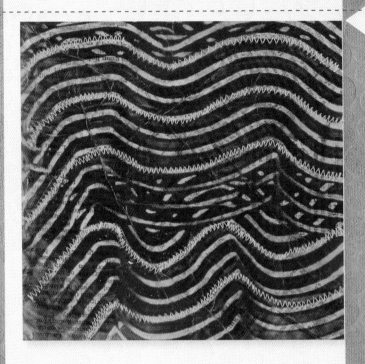

PASTE PAPER

Forget all those recipes for lumpy flour pastes. Pick up a tub of premixed wallpaper paste and you can use it for paper-cloth, plain paper, and fabric. Pour a little paste in a cup and add a squeeze of acrylic paint. Mix it up and spread it on the surface with a wide paintbrush. Comb, draw lines with your finger or a pencil end, or write text with the end of a paintbrush. Give it plenty of time to dry.

to create this piece: Spray yellow ink on the background. Add crimson paint to premixed wallpaper paste and brush a thick coat on the surface. Use a paintbrush handle to draw lines and waves in the paste and allow to dry well. Finish with coordinating thread in a zigzag stitch.

LIGHT MOLDING PASTE

Light molding paste is a fascinating concoction with the consistency of shaving cream and the spreadability of cake frosting. It looks edible, but don't be fooled. Light paste is flexible when dry but does better with a ground to adhere to, so prime the surface with some clear gesso first, and the paste will hold on tightly. Spread it with a palette knife. You can use it as is or in a stencil to create a raised design. Allow it to dry well before painting or staining.

to create this piece: Paint on deep purple textile color and blot with a rag. Apply light purple crackle paste and heat it until it dries and cracks appear. Lay down a stencil and use a palette knife to scrape light molding paste into the stencil pattern. Carefully remove the stencil and allow the molding paste to dry. Spray the surface with plum water-soluble ink. Apply Rub 'N Buff to the stenciled relief.

SPACKLE IMPASTO

When creating texture, the material you choose will depend on the ultimate use. Spackle will create fabulous impasto for artwork that is going to be firm and not subject to bending. For other projects, spread on light molding paste, which has the elasticity to hold up to movement and won't add any weight to the finished piece. Spread a layer of spackle with a palette knife, allowing the pattern of the strokes to show as if you were frosting a cake. Let it dry well before coloring, or add color directly to the paste before applying it.

to create this piece: Spread a very thin layer of spackle paste or light molding paste over the surface with a knife. Allow it to dry, then spray the surface with diluted acrylic paint in blue. Splatter white paint off a toothbrush to highlight.

EXPANDABLE PAINT

Expandable paint puffs up when heated and creates a truly unique surface. My favorite way to use it is through a stencil. Apply it over the stencil, remove it, and zap the paint with a heat gun. It will puff up and then shrink a little bit. Spritz inks over it when it's cool and let the color seep into the spaces between. Try rubbing metallic highlights on the tops of the raised areas.

to create this piece: Apply yellow fluid acrylic to the background. Use a stencil to apply expandable medium thickly, then remove the stencil. Apply a heat gun to cause the paint to puff up and harden. Spritz ink in butterscotch and espresso over the stenciled paint. Brush a little Rub 'N Buff over the high points with your finger. Add decorative bubble stitching with a free-motion machine stitch.

TAPING

Duct tape jokes aside, this generation is the lucky recipient of many useful and attractive tapes. Electrical tape now comes in neon brights. Each tape has its own properties, and I'll leave it to you to test them out in your own mixed media. Simple masking tape is a safe addition to surfaces, and it has a different rate of paint absorption, so it adds texture and interest when used on paper-cloth.

to create this piece: Sponge the paper-cloth with white shoe polish and spray it with plum water-based ink. Wait until it's very dry, then apply masking tape in a random pattern. Spray with ink again, then apply white paint to a sponge and dab it over the surface. Stitch the tape with purple thread.

GEL MEDIUM

Technically, you can add your own goodies to acrylic mediums, but why not let the good art doctor take the worry out of it? Gel mediums come with beads, sand, flakes, and lava. Their textures are pure joy to work with, and they remain flexible, too. Because they dry clear, they don't interfere with previous layers.

to create this piece: Brush on orange acrylic paint and allow it to dry. Dip a dry brush into red paint and run it across the page, leaving brush marks, then repeat. Stitch a grid with a fancy stitch and matching thread. Apply a random layer of gel medium with beads and allow to dry. Dab on orange, yellow, and nickel azo fluid acrylics, allowing the paint to seep into the crevices. Apply some gold metallic paint to a sponge and brush it over the highlights.

FUSIBLE FILM

Textiva is the fusible film that is the source of angelina. It's a clear, iridescent, crinkly film. It bubbles and shrinks when heated for an unusual textural effect. You can lay out the sheets of film and stitch them directly to the paper-cloth, leaving them that way, or you can heat them to melt away in sections. I've seen it used in a number of inventive ways—there is no right or wrong way to do things when a new mixed-media material is introduced.

to create this piece: Dab purple-blue textile paint on the background and sponge with a paper towel. On a separate piece of red paper-cloth, lay out a piece of fusible film and stitch a heart. Stitch a grid pattern in the center of the heart. With a craft knife, cut small slits in the fusible film. Use a heat gun to melt the fusible film back and curl it up. Cut out the heart and use fabric glue to attach it to the background. Stitch around the heart and stitch wings with pink thread.

MASKING AND RESISTS

Masking and resists have many applications in mixed media. With masking, you can apply several images without them overlapping each other, thereby creating a montage of images. You can also mask the edges of an image to produce a defined frame. Resists are similar in that they also prevent the coloring of specific areas within your creation. Both are easy techniques to master, and there are several ways to execute each one.

MASKING

Masking is the reverse of stamping. When you use a mask, everything that it covers is not printed with colorant and all else is. You can mask with a variety of paper shapes or even whole objects, such as leaves. Lay masks down on the paper-cloth, then apply color with spray paint or ink. Remove the masked shapes or try switching them to another location and respraying with a different color. For an easy mask, use masking tape. Its name even implies its primary purpose!

to create this piece: Color the background with a pink walnut ink dabber. Apply masking tape in a grid pattern. Sponge on dark crimson acrylic paint and allow to dry. Remove the tape, then accent the squares with metallic thread. Dab with embossing fluid and sprinkle on ultra-thick embossing enamel. Melt the embossing enamel with a heat gun, taking care not to singe the thread.

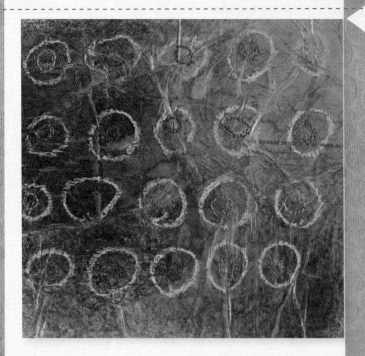

WAX RESIST

Do you remember those Easter egg kits that came with a colorless wax crayon? At my house we spent hours drawing greetings and childlike flowers on the eggs before dipping them in the vinegar-scented dye. That process is alive and well. Wax creates a great resist for mixed media. If you can't find the plain varieties, use regular crayons and melt them off with an iron and paper towel when you're done.

to create this piece: Color the background with yellow ink. Use a clear wax crayon, or a lightly colored one, to draw circles. Spray with water-based ink in butterscotch and allow it to dry. Use a heat gun to melt the wax and rub it off with a paper towel. Stitch circles with thread.

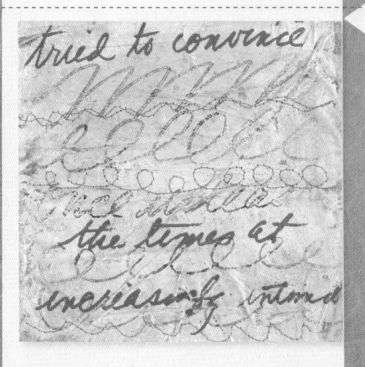

CLEAR RESIST EMBOSSING

Embossed areas are nonporous, shiny, and slick, so they resist paint and ink. Color the background first, then emboss designs with clear embossing enamel. They will allow the first color to show through but resist anything applied on top.

to create this piece: Color the background with persimmon shimmering spray color. Write and doodle with an embossing pen. Sprinkle on clear embossing powder and tap to remove the excess. Heat the surface to melt and emboss. Apply a wash of diluted white paint, allow to partially dry, then wipe off the embossed area.

PRINTMAKING TECHNIQUES

Believe it or not: printmaking is an easy and fun way to find serendipity. The four techniques below most likely can be accomplished with supplies you already have, and none of them require any more skill than a steady hand.

STENCILING

You can purchase premade stencils or create your own from plastic sheets or freezer paper. The plastic sheets (for sale alongside traditional stencils) are designed for cutting or burning with a heat tool. You make a template by drawing or printing out the design, then place it under the plastic sheet, tape it down, and cut out the areas with a craft knife. If you choose to use a woodburning tool, make sure the surface underneath can take the heat. With freezer paper, just print or draw your image on the non-waxy side, place the sheet on top of a cutting mat, and cut out the design with a craft knife. Iron the sheet to the paper-cloth surface and carefully peel off when finished for reuse.

to create this piece: Wash the surface with peach pearlescent ink. Use sequin waste as stencils to make dots, starting with deep blue paint, then adding white. Stitch around some of the circles with blue thread.

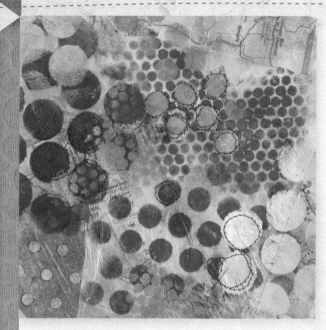

MONOPRINTING

A monoprint can be created only once, and essentially, it is akin to pulling a painted print. First, you need a hard, flat surface, such as an acrylic sheet. Then, use thick opaque paints to paint a design on the flat surface (monotype printing inks are available, but heavy acrylics work well). You can also brayer the ink onto the acrylic sheet and draw into it using a paint-

brush, pencil, or skewer. Once satisfied, lay the paper-cloth onto the plate and burnish it with your hand or a brayer. Pull the print and allow to dry.

to create this piece: *Use a brayer to roll a layer of paint on the acrylic sheet. With the end of a pencil, draw a design in the paint. Gently place the surface to be printed face down on the paint. Anchor the paper-cloth along one edge and slowly pull the print away from the acrylic sheet. Apply purple india ink with a sponge, then spray the surface with water and blot off ink. Cut a rectangle of orange paper-cloth for the monoprint. Use a brayer to spread out a layer of white paint on a sheet of clear acrylic. With your finger, draw a heart, removing the paint from the acrylic sheet. Place the orange paper-cloth face down on the heart and roll over it with a clean brayer. Peel the orange piece off to reveal the monoprint. Stitch around the heart with orange thread and sew on a button.*

LACE PRINTING

This method can be used with lace, cheesecloth, and any other fabric with a lot of open areas. Depending on the thickness of the lace, try rolling the painted brayer over it as a stencil, applying paint to the paper-cloth below. If it's thick, apply the paint to the lace and then place the lace face down on the surface and roll over it with the brayer to create a print.

to create this piece: *Collage the background with painted news-paper. Load a brayer with orange paint and roll it over a piece of lace. Lay the lace face down on the paper-cloth and use the brayer to press it well and make a print. Remove the lace.*

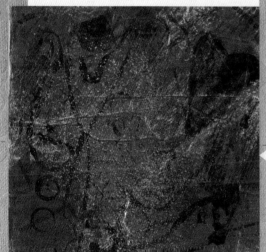

COLLAGRAPH PRINTING

To create a collagraph print, collage a group of dimensional items to a piece of cardboard, allow to dry, brayer the collage with ink, and then evenly burnish onto a sheet of paper-cloth. You can cut shapes from tag board, or you can search around the house for items to use, just be sure all of the chosen items have a relatively flat surface and are about the same height.

to create this piece: *Cut a piece of cardboard to serve as the base of your printing place. Squeeze out some craft glue and spread it around on the surface. Lay down string, buttons, safety pins, fabric, metal objects, etc. When the glue is dry, use a brayer to coat the surface with blue paint. Place the paper-cloth face down on top of the plate and use the brayer to roll over. Spray with red ink and blot dry.*

EFFECTS

I consider effects anything such as distressing or surfaces that have kind of an urban feel to them. They can also be transfers. What follows are eight techniques that can make your paper-cloth truly unique.

PEELED PAINT

Start by staining the background with ink or paint and allowing it to dry. Then use your finger to smear petroleum jelly on the surface. Don't cover all of it; just areas where you'd like the final paint to "peel away." Apply a coat of paint, working quickly so that you don't get the jelly on your brush. The top coat should form a nice contrast with the background, so use a light color if your background is dark and vice versa. Let the paint dry for a reasonable amount of time. Wipe the petroleum off with paper towels, taking the top layer of paint with it. The result is a surface that looks weathered and shabby.

to create this piece: Painting the background with purple textile glazing paints. Pick up some petroleum jelly with your finger and smear it on the surface, leaving some areas dry. Wash some diluted white paint quickly over the surface without moving the petroleum jelly. Allow the paint to dry, then wipe off the petroleum jelly, leaving a peeled-paint look. Fill a piece of freezer paper with dabs and streaks of paint in a rainbow of colors. Allow it to dry, then add more colors, building up a complex palette, then repeat. Stamp with large foam stamps, then cut it into shapes and glue it to the paper-cloth. Add some letter stickers.

RIPPED EDGE

Achieving a ripped edge on paper-cloth is a little trickier than with fabric, but it can be done. Make a snip with scissors to get the tear started and make sure you've cut into the fabric. The ripping will follow the line of the textile and take the paper along for the ride. One side will have the ragged edge you're trying for, so keep that side in your hand and pull the other strip away from you. If you end up with an edge that has fabric showing, sponge it with some matching paint.

to create this piece: Wash the background with pearlescent pink paint. Rip strips of paper-cloth and glue them to the surface with fabric glue. Top stitch them with contrasting thread in a wave pattern.

GRAFFITI

Often, graffiti conveys the feeling of one message over another in a never-ending revolution of communication. The major components are spray paint, stencils, and big, bold text. It's easy to achieve that look with stamps and stencils. When you use letter stencils, keep both the positive and the negative parts. Try laying down geometric shapes, spray painting over them, and then removing them.

to create this piece: Color the background by spraying it with green water-based ink. Apply some triangle stickers, spray paint with silver, then remove the stickers. Stamp various-sized letters randomly with blue, green, yellow, and shades in between.

RUST EMBOSS

I was pretty excited when I stumbled across rust-finish embossing powder. My whole family knows that I am a rustaholic. If it's rusty, I adore it. What could be better than applying a rusty finish at will? And to fabric no less!

to create this piece: Rub a walnut ink dabber over the paper-cloth surface to coat it. Ink up a foam stamp with embossing fluid and stamp a repeat pattern. Sprinkle on distress rust embossing powder and tap the surface to remove the excess. Melt the powder with a heat gun. Stitch around the embossing with matching thread.

ALTERED PHOTO

Altered photographs can be stitched or glued to many projects. To alter a photograph, simply sand the edges to give it a worn look, add a tint of alcohol ink, rip it, paint over it, cut it up. Your options are endless. For a surreal effect, use a paintbrush to cover the entire photo with alcohol ink.

to create this piece: Sponge on black acrylic paint and rub some of it off. Stamp circles with gold paint. Choose a photo and sand the edges with coarse sandpaper. Drip alcohol inks around the edges and wipe off with a paper towel. Glue the photo to the background with gel medium and stitch it down with gold thread.

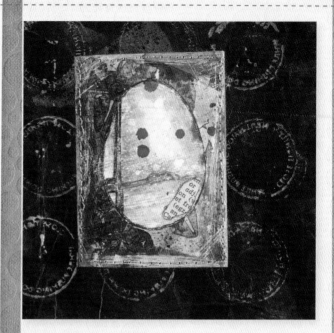

FABRIC FOIL

For shiny and warm or steely surfaces, foils come in a happy choice of metallic colors, including rainbow sheets. They are extremely easy to use. Although foil glue is available, I prefer to use either fusible web or bonding powder, depending on the effect I am trying to achieve. Fusible web will adhere larger areas of foil. Bonding powder comes in a shaker. You don't need much, so sprinkle it lightly. Either way, lay the foil sheet down on top of the fusible adhesive with the shiny, foiled side up. Because this is so counterintuitive, most of us have tried the other way first, only to be frustrated! Use a nonstick sheet to protect your iron and iron on a hot setting for a few seconds. Let it cool before pulling away the foil sheet.

to create this piece: Color the background with golden ink and splatter with shades of brown diluted paint. Ink up a foam stamp with bronze ink and stamp images on the paper-cloth. Outline stitch the elements with yellow thread. Cut some snippets of thin fusible web and lay them on the surface. Cover them with a piece of fabric foil, shiny side up. Place a nonstick sheet over both and iron well, allow to cool, and remove the foil sheet.

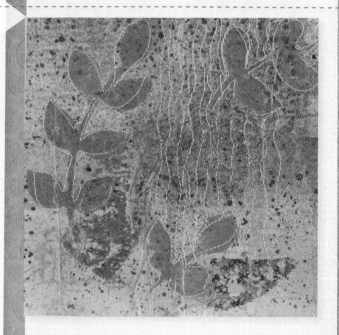

TAPE TRANSFER

The word "transfer" can make some of us cringe. Tape transfers, however, are easy, reliable, and inexpensive. If you've got a roll of clear packing tape and a sink, you're in business. The transfer will take to magazine images or photocopies in color or black and white. But don't try this with an ink-jet print. It won't work. When you're done, the tape transfer will be slightly sticky, but probably not enough to be useful, so use a little bit of gel medium or some vellum tape to adhere it to a surface.

to create this piece: Sponge peach acrylic paint to fill the background. Use orange and brown art markers to journal text and stitch around some of the text. Make a small color photocopy of an image, cover it with clear packing tape, and burnish it well. Place the tape in water for a few minutes, then rub off the paper to reveal the transfer. Apply it to the paper-cloth with a little gel medium and stitch around the elements with thread. Highlight with orange oil pastels.

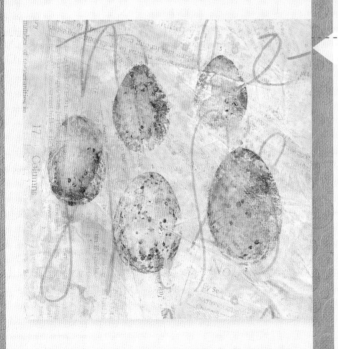

ACETONE TRANSFER

Because acetone evaporates quickly, it's one of the easier solvents to work with. Many nail-polish removers are acetone-based with added fragrance, and they will work for this process if you don't have a can of acetone solvent.

to create this piece: Sponge the background with mint green acrylic paint and spritz with green water-based ink. Place a black photocopy face down on the surface. Dip a cotton ball in acetone and rub the back of the image to wet it. Burnish the image for twenty seconds with a bone folder, then remove the paper. Splatter gold metallic paint on the surface with a bristle brush.

CRAFTED WHIMSY
POTENT PARTNERING OF TECHNIQUES AND MATERIALS WILL ADD EVEN MORE WONDER

Individually, each technique and supply offers marvelous opportunities, but together they can transform paper-cloth into something special. Partner methods and materials to take your artwork to a new level.

TAILORING

Paper-cloth has all the properties of fabric, so it is only natural to employ fabric techniques when working with it. Keep in mind that paper-cloth will be a little more firm than fabric yet also can be more delicate. It is a good idea to experiment with with plain paper-cloth to see which techniques you prefer.

APPLIQUÉ

Appliqué is a traditional quilting method in which pieces of fabric are cut and stitched on top of another layer of fabric. Ultimately, all of my appliquéd pieces are stitched to the under layer, but it is helpful to glue them down first to aid in stitching. Glue sticks work well if you are planning to stitch soon. If it's going to be a while or you're going to be handling the art a lot before stitching, it's better to use fabric glue for a stronger bond. Cut the pieces for your appliqué, arrange them and glue them down. Then either machine stitch or handstitch around them, close to the edge.

to create this piece: (portion shown here, full piece shown on page 22) Start with a 12" W x 12" H (30.5 x 30.5 cm) background of white paper-cloth. Cut circles and rings from colored paper-cloth with a circle cutter. Move them around until you find a pleasing arrangement, then glue them down and over stitch. Add more

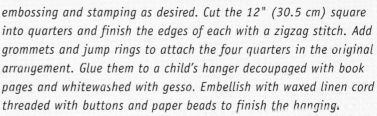

embossing and stamping as desired. Cut the 12" (30.5 cm) square into quarters and finish the edges of each with a zigzag stitch. Add grommets and jump rings to attach the four quarters in the original arrangement. Glue them to a child's hanger decoupaged with book pages and whitewashed with gesso. Embellish with waxed linen cord threaded with buttons and paper beads to finish the hanging.

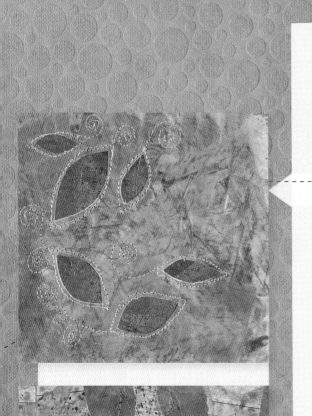

REVERSE APPLIQUÉ

In reverse appliqué, portions are cut away, revealing another layer and color of paper-cloth below. Draw the image you want to remove on the back of the sheet of paper-cloth. Use a sharp craft knife and cut over a self-healing mat. Audition different colors of paper-cloth underneath the cut-away areas until you find a combination that works. Place the new material behind the window and stitch around it to attach it. Trim the excess.

to create this piece: Collage with vintage correspondence. Brush with pink twinkling watercolors and spray with gold shimmer ink. Use a craft blade to cut leaf shapes out of the surface. Use fabric glue to attach orange paper-cloth underneath. Machine stitch lime green thread around the leaves and in a swirl pattern.

CONTRAST STITCHING

Choose contrasting colors of thread and paper-cloth to make a vivid statement and emphasize the stitching.

to create this piece: Collage on map pieces. Spray with orange diluted paint, then over stamp with orange acrylic and foam stamps. Splatter the background with blue paint. Use a craft knife to cut out some squares. Use fabric glue to attach blue paper-cloth behind the squares. Glue the removed orange squares between the blue squares. Cut smaller squares of orange and blue paper-cloth and center them in the big squares. Stitch with orange and blue thread.

COUCHING FIBERS

It's easy to add softness and color to the surface of paper-cloth with fancy art fibers. Use invisible or clear monofilament thread and a zigzag stitch to attach them.

to create this piece: Spray purple water-based ink on the background and blot it dry. Add some butterscotch ink and blot. Lay out gem-toned fiber and fasten it to the surface with a zigzag stitch and translucent thread. As you move across the paper-cloth, mold the fiber in a free-form pattern, stitching as you go.

EMBROIDERY

I enjoy the feel of handstitching. It adds a special quality of care and attention to detail. When I make paper quilts, I love to save the embroidery for last. There are fabulous hand-dyed flosses available as well, adding to the charm. Use the smallest needle you can get away with, as the larger the needle, the larger the hole in the paper-cloth.

to create this piece: *Brush on red fabric paint to cover the background. With fabric glue, add a photo image and overlap the edges with more red paint. Stitch around the image with several colors of matching thread. Journal some text with a black permanent marker. Use an un-threaded sewing machine to stitch squares on the surface to perforate. Hand embroider around the image with a straight stitch.*

FELTING

Needlefelting can be done by hand with a single needle or a multi-needle device, or it can be done by machine. For our purposes, any kind of roving or fiber will do, including art fibers and yarns. A felting needle or a felting machine has no thread. Instead, the roving fibers are pushed through to the back of the fabric, where they become entangled with the other fibers. This action is re-peated until the fibers meld with the fabric, or, in this case, the paper-cloth. Be careful not to make too many punctures in the paper-cloth. Keep the needles over the roving and avoid traveling on to the bare paper-cloth.

to create this piece: *Collage with book text and brush on pink textile paint. Stitch free-motion circles with pink thread and a sewing machine. Lay out tufts of corn fiber roving in orange, pink, and purple and felt them with a felting machine. Add hand-embroidered elements with purple metallic floss.*

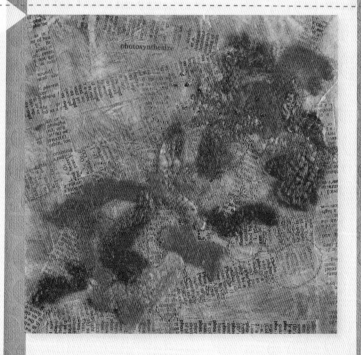

QUILTING

When quilting, the only thing to consider is that the paper surface makes mistakes apparent. So as long as care is taken, quilting on paper-cloth is a happy circumstance. You can quilt on batting or felt, but the surface is stiffer so it will not have the same effect that quilting to batting would have on fabric. Things won't look quite as quilted, since the surface is static. You can, however, use any of the free-motion or fancy machine stitches you use elsewhere. Constant check of your settings will be necessary, as thicknesses vary considerably from one paper-cloth to another. Change the tension if necessary, particularly since you don't want to be ripping out stitching later. As a personal choice, I keep my free-motion foot on at least 80 percent of the time, preferring to stitch around most elements as if I were drawing with the thread.

to create this piece: Roll pink textile paint over the paper cloth with a brayer and allow it to dry. With matching pink thread, stitch a series of waves.

CRAZY QUILTING

Crazy quilting is recycling scraps and pieces of re-purposed fabric for quilts. You can use fancy machine stitches or stick to a simple zigzag stitch to attach elements. Trim ragged edges before you use each piece. Slightly overlap one piece over another and top stitch them together. Add another piece of paper-cloth and stitch where it overlaps both of the other pieces. Work out from the center, adding pieces and stitching them together until you create a large piece of whole cloth. Now you're ready to cut it up for projects.

to create this piece: Gather scraps of paper-cloth and begin zigzag stitching them together with black thread. Form a sheet of crazy-quilted paper-cloth and cut it up for projects.

FABRIC LAYERING

Use fabric glue to add more layers of dyed, stamped, or printed cloth to the paper-cloth base. You can stitch multiple layers, alternating paper and cloth.

to create this piece: *Sponge the background with green pearlescent ink. Stitch diamonds with green variegated thread. Rubber stamp elements with pink paint. Sandwich thin fusible web between a page of book text and sheet of sheer fabric. Cover with a nonstick sheet and iron gently to fuse but not to melt the fabric. Drip and blot ink on the surface. Iron some smaller strips of fusible web onto the fabric, remove the backing, and iron on fabric foil. Cut the fabric into a heart shape and stitch it onto the paper-cloth. Use an oil pastel to draw around the heart.*

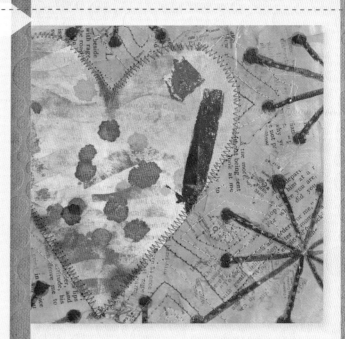

ANGELINA FIBERS

Loose fibers can be used as is and felted with wool or silk, or they can be made into sheets for cutting into shapes. Additionally, you can use fusible web to iron them directly to the surface of fabric or paper-cloth. To make a sheet of angelina, place some tufts between a folded nonstick sheet and iron very briefly. If you iron it too long, it will lose its iridescence. Cut the sheets into shapes.

to create this piece: *Spray the background with orange ink. Stamp it with pink paint and a foam stamp. Rub white gesso on top to highlight some areas. Stitch swirls with pink thread. Place some tufts of angelina fibers between a folded nonstick sheet and iron briefly to form a sheet. Cut petal shapes and stitch them to the paper-cloth with iridescent thread. Add beads by hand.*

JOURNALING

Most people are shy about their handwriting, but often our own cursive scrawls offer the most character. If you are unsure about your writing, practice what you want to write first. You can see from my work that I am a fan of the unreadable scribble, as it conveys the feel of meaning, without the distraction of a secondary message. I will write on anything, and if I'm not writing words, I'm happy stamping random letters. For me, art without text is mute.

PAINT-PEN JOURNALING

To journal, begin writing about something you're interested in or some process you are familiar with. You can journal the lyrics to a song or repeat the chatter on the radio. Write down a recipe or your thoughts about the season. Anything works when you are creating paper-cloth to be cut up in projects. If you are journaling on a finished piece of artwork, you'll have to be more intentional about what you write, designing it to fit with the theme of the piece.

to create this piece: Wash the background with yellow fluid acrylics. Place dabs of green and blue paint on a brayer and roll it over the surface. Stamp swirls with blue paint and free stitch around them with a sewing machine. With a white paint pen, write a journal entry.

THREAD SKETCHING

Thread sketching—free-motion stitching around images with thread—is one of my favorite art processes. Sketching with black thread replicates the look of pen sketching, but you can also use colored thread. The idea is to make it look dashed off and casual, so work as fast as you can without veering off course. Don't make the lines perfect. Some things look great if you go over them more than once. You can also "write" with the sewing machine, using a cursive script to flow from one letter to the next and breaking between words. Don't over think it. Imperfection is uniquely delightful.

to create this piece: Brush peach pearl acrylic ink on the background and drip darker ink. Journal text with a blue art marker. Use a matching blue thread to free-motion stitch around the text.

STAMPED TEXT

I simply cannot pass up a new alphabet stamp set, particularly when it's new to me but a vintage find. Practice, practice, practice, which means stamp once on scrap paper before stamping directly on the surface. It's hard to undo mistakes, so go slowly. Read twice, stamp once, to reword a famous quote. A piece of material is not a ledger, so things don't have to be linear. Stamp your text in any direction that pleases you. Mix up letter sizes and cases to keep the text light and off-balance.

to create this piece: *This paper-cloth was created with joss paper. Stamp various sizes of foreign characters in orange and black paint. Stamp journaled text across the front.*

BAUBLES AND MORE

Dimension can be the ultimate finishing touch for your paper-cloth. You can travel down any number of paths to achieve dimension, but a few great places to start are your junk drawer, jewelry box, and basket of sewing notions.

BUTTONS AND FOUND OBJECTS

Buttons and found objects can be glued or stitched to a paper-cloth base, depending on how secure they need to be. Buttons and cloth are made for each other, after all, and vintage mother-of-pearl buttons are wonderful reminders of an enchanted world gone by. Try sewing on a variety of flat objects, like sequins, dyed washers, or charms.

to create this piece: *Sponge the background with purple pearlescent ink. Use craft glue to attach buttons to the front. Dab purple, terra-cotta, and red alcohol inks on the buttons with a small brush. Sprinkle gold TroCol powder on some of the buttons. Stamp dots with purple acrylic and sprinkle more TroCol powder.*

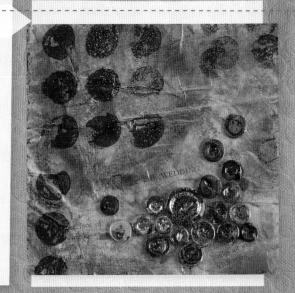

BEADING

Nearly all fabric treatments are appropriate for paper-cloth, including beading. Seed beads and others add a lovely, dimensional quality to paper-cloth quilts and projects. Use a beading needle and fine beading thread, just as you would for cloth.

to create this piece: Collage a portrait with different sheets of paper-cloth and affix with fabric glue. Stitch around the pieces to finish. Add seed beads with beading floss and a needle.

STAPLING

There are many decorative staples on the market now. Some are bright colors and others have designs etched into them. Far beyond their basic utilitarian purpose, they are pretty enough to be a decorative element. Try stapling paper or fabric scraps to your paper-cloth background.

to create this piece: Collage on squares of book text with diluted glue or gel medium. Wash the background with orange india ink. Use a foam stamp and green acrylic to stamp a design. Spritz a piece of canvas with gold ink and allow it to dry. Rip small squares from the fabric and staple them to the surface with colored staples.

INSPIRATION STATION
USE THESE EXERCISES TO LIGHT YOUR CREATIVE FIRE

We are all full of creativity, sometimes we just need a little help harnessing our power. If you are on the brink of brilliance, but need a little nudge over the edge, perhaps some of the following activities will help set your juice loose.

SAY WHAT?

I'm an aphorism hoarder, and the list below is merely a sampling of my favorite quotes. I thought it might be fun to include a little matching exercise. Read the quote and see if you can correctly match its originator. Fun activities are a great way to keep thinking about creativity without trying to compel yourself to produce something creative. So, please, sit back, read, and let the mind wander to other lands for a minute. The answers are just under your nose. No, not there . . . inside the book, to the right, at the bottom.

1. ". . . you don't reach Serendib by plotting a course for it. You have to set out in good faith for elsewhere and lose your bearings . . . serendipitously."

2. "This discovery, indeed, is almost of that kind which I call Serendipity, a very expressive word, which, as I have nothing better to tell you, I shall endeavor to explain to you: you will understand it better by the derivation than by the definition. I once read a silly fairy tale, called *The Three Princes of Serendip*; as their Highnesses traveled, they were always making discoveries, by accidents and sagacity, of things which they were not in quest of."

3. "To invent you need a good imagination and a pile of junk."

4. "You cannot use up creativity. The more you use, the more you have."

5. "If you want to make an apple pie from scratch, you must first create the universe."

6. "The best way to have a good idea is to have lots of ideas."

7. "You need chaos in your soul to give birth to a dancing star."

8. "The hand is the visible part of the brain."

9 "Do not worry about your originality. You could not get rid of it even if you wanted to."

10 "Take an object. Do something to it. Do something else to it. Ditto."

11 "Generally speaking, color directly influences the soul. Color is the keyboard, the eyes are hammers, the soul is the piano with many strings. The artist is the hand that plays, touching one or another purposively, to cause vibrations in the soul."

12 "Art is created through intuition."

13 "The route of my pencil on the sheet of paper is, in some respects, analogous to the gesture of a man groping in darkness . . . I am led, I do not lead."

14 "All truly profound art requires its creator to abandon himself to certain powers which he invokes but cannot altogether control."

15 "Chaos is inherent in all compounded things. Strive on with diligence."

16 "Every artist dips his brush in his own soul, and paints his own nature into his pictures."

17 "Beginnings are always messy."

a. Maya Angelou	j. Linus Pauling
b. Jasper Johns	k. Thomas Edison
c. Nietzsche	l. John Galsworthy
d. Andre Malraux	m. Henri Matisse
e. Buddha	n. Henry Ward Beecher
f. Piet Mondrian	o. Carl Sagan
g. Immanuel Kant	p. Robert Henri
h. John Barth	q. Horace Walpole
i. Wassily Kandinsky	

Answers:
1-h, 2-q, 3-k, 4-a, 5-o, 6-j, 7-c, 8-g, 9-p, 10-b, 11-i, 12-f, 13-m, 14-d, 15-e, 16-n, 17-l

CREATIVE SPELLS

Looking to cast a little magic? These will do the trick. As I wrote this book, I wondered if giving the recipes for all of my paper-cloth swatches would take the serendipitous fun away from my readers. On the other hand, I also wanted to be sure that my readers would be able to re-create my paper-cloth examples if they so desired. Really, how frustrating to purchase a how-to book without the how-to. The solution to my problem lies on the next four pages—exercises aimed at helping you get started without telling you where to go.

PHOTO FINISH

Print out a favorite photo on plain paper. Use a marker or pen to trace just the primary lines and elements in the drawing. Make a painting or collage, using these shapes as a guide.

GATHER COLOR

Keep a color journal. Whenever you see color combinations that make your artistic spirit sing, take a photo or print them out and paste them into your color journal. Systematically make artwork that uses these color combos.

SWATCH-O-RAMA

Make your own paint swatches with the materials and mediums you have in your studio. Cut some watercolor paper into strips, slather on some paint, and note the formula underneath. Make swatches of similar colors or combinations you like. Create a "signature" series of swatches with colors you like to work in.

GO TONAL

When in doubt about a color scheme, go tonal. Choose a single color, then use variations for effect. Add white and gray to make lighter and darker versions, or use water or glaze to thin or change the properties. It's amazing what you can do with one color!

CHECK IT OUT

Go to your public library and check out some books on collage, color theory, altered art, and paint effects. Take notes. Find out if they have any online books about creativity and self-expression. Your library can be an endless source of inspiration and yummy ideas.

COLOR WHEELIN'

Don't discount the value of color theory. There's no need to go back to school. Purchase a simple color wheel and hang it up where you can see it while you work. If you find that something needs a little extra punch, try adding a bit of the color showing opposite on the wheel (complementary color).

FABRIC BOOK

Find an old book you're not using and make it into a common book of fabrics. Staple squares of your favorite fabrics to the pages, then try to match the colors with the paints you have on hand. Look at the patterns and carve your own rubber stamps to match.

BAR THE BLANK

The blank page is intimidating for artists and writers alike. Bar the blank page by creating some colorful backgrounds that will inspire you. Use any of the techniques in this book to create a presence on journal pages or white canvas. It's not as scary to make that first mark, when the page is already started for you.

There is nothing worse than idling your muse because you can't think of what to create. Join in an online swap, especially one you've never tried before. This will force you to work through a project and learn a new skill. When you are finished, you will have expanded your repertoire, and you may find a new passion (or better, a friend). Many of my favorite techniques were derived while trying to meet a swap deadline.

If necessity is the mother of invention, what is the father? It may be forgetting. Try forgetting the "proper" way to use art supplies and just play with them. Hold your brush or pen in the wrong hand and see what happens. Instead of drawing a picture and then painting it, try brushing paint on the canvas and then outlining the shapes with a marker. Lose your brushes and try to find new ways to get paint on the paper. Be a caveman artist (for more caveman artist ideas, see below).

thE found "Brush" discover unique painting and drawing tools in your yard, home, and office

Today's wide selection of shaped brushes with handles, ferrules, and bristles is a modern invention. Our ancestors used whatever was on hand to render their artistic commentary. To inspire a new perspective, allow your environment to refresh your creative mind. Look around you and begin experimenting with a variety of fun, found items that you can use to draw, paint, and stamp on your designs. If you plan to reuse the found brush for its intended purpose, make sure it is easily washable.

nature

Mother Nature's paintbrushes ofttimes are already filled with pigment. Take advantage of textures, tips, and the wonderful colors these items can add to your work.

* Twigs, rocks, and leaves have wonderful, tangible textures that can leave distressed, streaky, and mottled effects.
* Flowers and grasses with unusual shapes could act as stamps or delicate paintbrushes.
* Zesty vegetables and fruits have interesting textures and designs both inside and out. Try carving a potato into a stamp or edging your paper-cloth with a ruby red beet.
* Decorative grasses or leaves can be dipped in paint for use as a natural brush.

home

One could spend an afternoon identifying household items that could be artfully repurposed. Below are a few ideas to ignite your mind, but don't overlook toothpicks, utensils, toothbrushes, plastic wrap, rags, lids, packaging, combs, and buttons.

* Trash can be treasure. Take a good hard look at what's headed for the trash. Packaging and worn-out gadgets often yield an abundance of funky surfaces for printing.
* A natural bristle hairbrush can be wanded across a paper-cloth sheet for an interesting color wash. Or, try using a toothbrush to splatter paint.

office

Your desk is a treasure chest of art supplies: bubble wrap, paper clips, pencils, erasers, sticky notes, coffee cups—all can be used with ingenuity.

* Paper clips have funky little designs that can be used as masks. Sprinkle some paper clips onto the paper-cloth and sponge over them with paint. Once the paint is dry, remove the clips for a fascinating little design.
* Lint rollers, of all things, have lots of potential. Gather small random objects and adhere them to the roller. Apply a bit of paint and roll out a design.

thROUGH a MICROSCOPE
See the trees that inhabit your creative forest

Creativity often consumes us in the big picture, leaving us too concerned with the final result. Yet, time taken to nurture the smallest of elements will be rewarded with rich visual content and unanticipated pleasures. As you construct your paper-cloth, relish in the details.

subtlety

Under a microscope it's clear to see that nature builds complex forms, layer upon layer. Take a cue from the cosmos and leave something to the viewer's imagination.

* Partially obscured text and images encourage a closer view. Use tissue paper, gesso, or paint to cover portions of the background or use water to unearth the original layer.

* A hidden message imparts mystique. Write your thoughts in large flowing script across the sheet so that each smaller piece provides just enough text to pique curiosity.

* Monochromatic elements that blend into the background make the most of nature's camouflage effect. Try printing with many different stamps dipped in the same color paint.

variety

It's true that no two snowflakes are alike. Similarly, each piece of serendipitously created artwork is utterly unique. Celebrate variety with a potpourri of formulas culled from your own art stash. No license is required to use art supplies in unconventional ways.

* Diversity can spring from quantity. Instead of using one technique, use three or five.

* It's okay to think outside the thicket when combining materials. If you usually sponge it, spray it instead. If you generally brush it on, stamp it this time.

* Variety is the spice. Mix it up! Create a custom blend with a little bit of this and a little dab of that from your art pantry. Let your intuition guide you as you stir up a masterpiece.

complexity

The macro view reveals a range of textures, colors, and forms in a single leaf. This underlying complexity is not always obvious at first glance, but without it the forest would lose its sparkle.

* The juxtaposition of formal and informal elements creates tension. Create unexpected combinations by placing printed and hand-drawn components next to each other.

* A little asymmetry never hurt anyone. Close your eyes and create without reciting design principles. Abandon straight lines and create random patterns.

* Intricate detailing in the form of subtle texture or delicate stamped design are perfect finishing touches that invite the viewer to stay and linger for a while.

AMPLIFY

Exaggerate an element. Look at a photo, compose a still life of objects, or use a portrait. Choose one of the elements and make it larger, just for fun. This will serve to add a bit of whimsy to your art and throw off the mantle of the mundane.

CUPBOARD

Pick an item out of your cupboard and use it as a model for some projects. Choose the shape, the color, or the text to play with and envision it in different settings. Sketch, stitch, or collage the item in various poses. Art is not about the subject, it's about what you do with it. Anything can serve as inspiration, even a can of soup.

PLANT A PHOTO

Glue a photograph to the center of a piece of paper and use it as a seed. With a pen, begin extending the elements of the photo out onto the paper. Now color them in so that the photo becomes part of the drawing. Let the photo send its tendrils out onto the paper. When you're done, the photo should blend in and become invisible.

SHOW OFF YOUR SPIRIT

Show the world you're a free spirit, with your own artful shirt. Find a loose 100 percent cotton shirt at a thrift shop. Write on it with a permanent marker. Draw, doodle, and journal or add quotations. Now fill in the drawings with textile paints or acrylic paints with added textile medium. Iron the paintings when they're dry to set them. If you'd like, stitch around some of the drawings with thread. Sew on fancy buttons or charms. This shirt is for fun days, when you want to show the world you're an artist.

DICTIONARY DOWSING

Randomly poke your finger into the dictionary and write down the word you fall upon. Now draw or collage a visual representation of that word. Many words have multiple meanings, so address them all. If you had to make a quilt or a painting of this word, sketch what that would look like. I know it's silly, but it could happen.

ALPHABET SOUP

Write out each letter of the alphabet, then find an art supply or product in your stash that begins with each letter. If you skip Q, X, and Z no one but you will know. Now start a mixed-media collage and use each item from your alphabet list, from acrylic medium to zigzag stitching. Use them in order or pass "Go," and start over.

CATALOGING COLOR

Choose a color, then begin identifying all the things around you that represent that color. Draw and paint them or create a photo spread and paste it in your color journal. Walk around and find more items in that color range and document them. See how many different variations there are on a single color theme.

BREAK IT

Break away from the familiar and reset your patterns to spur creativity. Start a meal with dessert. Start conversations at the end and work toward the beginning. Break your routine.

PARROT ACT

Repetition is pleasing to most people. The familiarity of repeated shapes is reassuring. Make something that repeats a pattern across the page. Use a stamp or a photocopy to make multiple prints, then color or embellish each differently.

SCRAP BINGO

Get a shoebox and go through your studio or art space, picking up scraps and leftover bits. It's okay to take some from the trash! Make a collage from this random flotsam or sew them to a length of fabric and turn it into an art quilt.

creations

Designing wild and juicy papered fabrics is only the first step. Now it's time to unleash your vibrant materials, and let them live out their purpose. There is so much you can create with mixed-media paper-cloth, from pillows and dolls to jewelry and paper art quilts. Paper-cloth is sturdy, so don't be afraid to construct items that will be touched and explored. The art in this book is meant to be handled, and your own labors of love will give you reason to smile daily at your creative spark.

Most of the projects in this book require the use of a sewing machine and a variety of thread colors. There is plenty of room for embellishment with handstitching and embroidery, but the primary method of securing and finishing is by machine. A good pair of scissors and a bottle of fabric glue make up the remaining staples for projects. Everything else is up to you to adapt. I recommend unearthing those hidden treasures and special supplies you've been hoarding for a rainy day and spreading them out around you. Serendipity cannot work its magic unless you can see what's available. The best projects result from good materials, so don't hold back.

Each project will offer "raw elements," which are the basic materials you'll want to have on hand. From these come the inspiration for completing a project. The wonderful thing about the creative process is its easy adaptability to a range of styles and skills. I have no doubt that you can take these basic project plans and veer off into another wonderful direction that highlights your own artistic notions. Each time we sit down at the sewing machine or string a bead or sketch a flower, we are adding to our creative inventory. Feel free to invent as you go. These projects are the product of my own serendipitous experimentation, and I hope they spur you on in your own artistic journey. Just make art and the inspiration will surely follow.

fEstive los MUertos GREETINGS

I have long been fascinated by the festive Day of the Dead or *el Día de los Muertos* celebrations common to Mexico. Even our October 31st wedding was fashioned around that theme. The wedding cake was decorated with colorful candy skulls and topped with a traditional skeleton bride and groom, and each place setting featured a miniature gravestone.

It's appropriate to send greetings to the living while honoring the memory of those who have left us, and these greeting cards capture all the festivity of the occasion. They remind us to live each day to the fullest, embracing each facet of life and all the while smiling. Take the collaged greeting card concept in any direction by making birthday cards, thank you's, and more, or whip up some generic cards using leftover scraps of paper-cloth and fabric. Add some foil, beads, and charms to create a unique handmade greeting or stitch on a photo for a personalized "hello" anyone would be thrilled to receive.

Raw elements

black card stock or premade blank cards

assorted paper-cloth pieces

fabric glue

sewing machine

black thread

optional: rubber stamps, ink pads

CREATE

1   Fold the card stock in half to form a greeting card. Use black card stock or paint the front background black to better accent the paper-cloth colors.

2   Cut a rectangle of paper-cloth slightly smaller than the cover and attach it with fabric glue.

3   Cut a skull shape and affix it to the center, then add eyes, a nose, and a mouth cut out of paper-cloth. Embellish with hearts, flowers, swirls, and other tra-ditional Day of the Dead symbols. The Internet is full of Day of the Dead resources—research the imagery for visual inspiration.

4   Top stitch around the skull and shapes with a free-motion stitch. The stitching will be visible on the inside cover of the card, but that's fine—it tells the recipient that you care enough to make a work of art just for them.

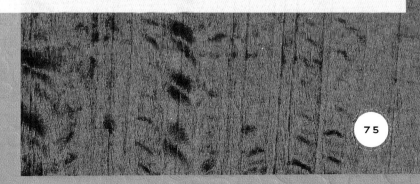

These free-form, all-occasion cards resulted from layering paper-cloth with fabric shapes and then stitching everything to attach. A stash of scraps will be handy for creating such cards on the fly.

Paper-cloth, card stock with stitching
4" W x 4" H (10.16 x 10.16 cm)

When asked to describe a spiral staircase, most people resort to making a spiral gesture with their hands. This is the perfect illustration of the dynamic between left and right brain thinking. When the left brain, charged with verbal processes, fails to offer a solution, the right brain kicks in—visualization and spatial relations are the realm of the right brain. The most creative people make use of a whole-brained approach, using both sides of the brain. It's easy to let yourself work on autopilot, but right brain/left brain exercises will help facilitate better functioning between both sides of your creative self, stimulating a new level of artistic dynamics.

RIGHT BRAIN

The right brain is a visual paradise, offering intuitive, nonlinear solutions that address the whole picture. Right-brain thinkers are expert at dealing with ambiguity, allowing them to inhabit the delightful spectrum of grays that bridge black and white. Feed intuition and perception by exercising this area of the brain.

GO TOPSY TURVY Encourage the right-brain view by working upside down. Turn an image 180 degrees and re-create it by seeing the lines and shapes, rather than the whole picture. When you're finished drawing, turn it right side up and see what your left brain says.

COLOR A WORD Is it possible to describe a word in visual terms? To the left brain, words have specific meanings that don't take into account how they make us feel. Exercise the right brain by writing down a word representing a complex idea, then translate it into a picture. Your finished artwork should invoke a tangible sense of meaning.

SING FOR SPONTANEITY Repetitive actions release creativity as they keep the left brain engaged in minor tasks. That's why your most creative time may be while you're brushing your teeth or showering. Sing out loud or repeat a "mantra" of any kind while working creatively to allow your right brain the freedom to be spontaneous. Speed readers use this trick to turn off that nagging left-brain voice.

IMAGINE A PHOTO Choose a photograph and identify the primary shapes represented by outlining them in marker. If you had to break it down into three or five basic areas, what would they be? Create an abstract painting or quilt based on the shapes in the photo. Add in some of the minor shapes while keeping the image abstract. If it helps, use photo-manipulation software to begin the process.

LEFT BRAIN

The left brain is a verbal wonderland, awash in logic and order. In school we make the most of this type of thinking, focusing on reading, writing, and math. Left-brain thinkers are adept at finding order and making sure that none of the details are overlooked. Exercising this area of the brain means building neural pathways that speed the processing of information and solving problems through deductive reasoning. In art, the inner left-brain critic can help make sure that you are progressing in a logical way and that all the steps are in place. Encourage symmetry and order by exercising this area of the brain.

BE A CRITIC The left brain is the inner critic. Look at a piece of work by another artist and write a critical review as if you were crowned art reviewer for a day. What are the strengths and weaknesses? What could be done to improve the message? Focus on the techniques involved and not just the emotion.

APPLAUD YOUR SUPPLIES Explore the technical aspects of your art supplies by reading about them. Start with the information on the packaging, then look up resources like the manufacturer's website and artists' message sites. Find out what makes them tick and take a closer look.

PAINT WITH WORDS The idea that a picture paints a thousand words is lost on the left brain, which is why writing descriptively is a left-brain exercise. Choose a painting and employ as many adjectives to describe it so that your reader would end up with the same image in his or her mind. Have someone read your description and sketch it out to see if they arrive at the same conclusion.

STEP IT OUT List the steps you would take to re-create a famous work of art, whether the artist created it that way or not. It's comforting to the left brain to know that even wildly creative endeavors can be broken into manageable stages.

good fortune BIRDS

Everyone loves birds—they are such whimsical and fascinating creatures. Strands of birds are common throughout many cultures, and they hold loads of creative symbolism. A little online research will teach you that blue birds are significant of happiness and fulfillment, and cardinals symbolize the importance of being while crows are the image of intelligence, watchfulness, are magical, and can be used to show connections to past lives. Your birds can be created for the sake of beauty or you can imbue them with symbolism. Perhaps model your birds after Nepalese prayer flags and create each one with an intention you would like realized. Once finished, I like to hang them on my front door as a greeting or to create a mobile so they can twirl freely in the breeze. A small bell will ring in the good creative spirits while showing off my handiwork.

Raw elements

- card stock
- marker
- paper-cloth pieces
- ribbon 48" (122 cm) long for each bird strand
- fabric glue
- sewing machine
- thread
- permanent marker
- paints
- bell

CREATE

1 Make a simple bird template out of card stock or download a pattern from the Internet. Use the template or pattern to trace and cut ten bird shapes from paper-cloth—trace half facing one direction and half facing the other. Make each bird body about 6" (15.24 cm) long.

2 Cut wings, eyes, and beaks from other paper-cloth colors, attach them with a glue stick, then stitch them to the bird body.

3 Lay out a length of ribbon or string. Fold over the top and sew it to form a loop for hanging.

4 Beginning 6" (15.24 cm) from the top, place two bird bodies together with the ribbon in the center. Tack them in place with a glue stick and top stitch around each bird duo with a zigzag stitch. Measure 3" down from the bottom of the first bird and add another until you have added five sets of birds.

5 Attach a bell at the bottom and hang your good fortune birds.

crazy-quilted BOOKMARKS

Raw elements

crazy-quilted paper cloth
felt
sewing machine
thread
screw punch
assorted fibers

If you're like me, there is no such thing as too many bookmarks. I love to see my bookshelf spilling over with artwork that is holding my place until the next good read. These instructions are for a single bookmark, but I'm sure you'll want to make a baker's dozen to give away. It's a great way to use up all of your leftover paper-fabric scraps. Crazy-quilted paper-cloth makes a very sturdy base for a range of projects, including these funky bookmarks. Follow the instructions in chapter two to make a large piece of crazy-quilt material that you can cut into shapes. Although these bookmarks are traditional rectangles, you can cut them into hearts or other shapes as well. You can add the delicious art fibers or try the other options such as beads or buttons.

CREATE

1. Make a large piece of crazy-quilted paper-cloth, following the instructions on page 61. The larger the finished piece, the more bookmarks you can make.

2. Measure and cut bookmarks and matching felt backs to 2" W × 8" H (5 × 20.32 cm).

3. Top the felt back with crazy-quilted paper-cloth and stitch the edges together, using a zigzag, blanket, or other stitch of your choice.

4. Add decorative stitching with gold thread or cut and add paper-cloth shapes.

5. Use a screw punch to make a hole in the top center of the bookmark.

6. Thread a bunch of art fibers or waxed linen thread through the hole and knot them at the top. String with beads and buttons if desired.

To add a decorative touch to these bookmarks, try handstitching, writing text with a permanent marker or paint pen, or stamping and then embossing designs to the fronts.

A sweet way to commemorate your favorite food is with a glittery quilt inspired by cake. It's okay to use glitter or other nontraditional materials in art quilts.

12" W x 12" H (30.48 x 30.48 cm)

Use rubber stamps and acrylic paint to add easy text to your design. "Coffee and Cake" looks delicious when rendered in paper-cloth.

12" W x 12" H (30.48 x 30.48 cm)

arT formULas
Brew creativity from scratch

The quantity of art supplies brimming from store shelves seems to multiply daily. If you're overwhelmed by the list of "must-have" products, why not try making a few of your own homemade concoctions with supplies you have on hand?

add some sparkle

✱ Create your own glimmering colors of embossing powder by adding a dash of pigmented mica powder to clear embossing powder before use. Then stamp, sprinkle, and heat as usual.

✱ Make a shimmering raised design by drawing shapes with a hot glue gun, then rubbing on mica powder. Alternatively, create a wax seal by pressing a stamp inked with embossing fluid into a blob of hot glue. When cool, remove the stamp and rub with mica powders.

✱ Bottle your own radiant sprays by mixing a little mica powder into a spray bottle filled with diluted paint, ink, or just plain water.

✱ Add a pinch of Schminke powder to liquid watercolors or inks, then paint as usual for a sparkling effect.

juice up the color

✱ Recycle old, broken crayons to create rainbow writers. Place peeled, broken pieces of crayons in cupcake liners (five per liner). Heat at 350° F for a few minutes until they melt. When cool, peel off the liner and use your new coloring tool as is or cut it into strips.

✱ Create your own inexpensive alcohol ink with fabric dye and isopropyl alcohol. Simply dilute powdered or liquid fabric dye (Rit or Dylon works) with alcohol and shake or stir well to dissolve. Mix your own custom colors by combining dyes.

✱ If you don't have walnut ink, just brew some strong instant coffee and brush it on until you achieve the effect you desire. Alternatively, sprinkle on coffee crystals and spritz with water, then allow to dry before brushing off.

✱ If you like the look of clear color glazes but don't want to purchase a host of new colors, mix acrylic glaze medium with your paint. It will impart a lustrous translucence to regular acrylic paint colors.

add some pattern

✱ Mix up some quick and easy paste paper designs with premixed paste. Pour some pre-mixed wallpaper paste into a paper cup. Add a dribble of acrylic paint and stir. Brush on, then use a comb or fork to make a design and allow to dry.

✱ Make your own puffy paint. Combine equal amounts of flour, salt, and water. Add liquid paint. Pour the mixture into squeeze bottles and use them to make designs. When dry, the lines will be puffy.

✱ For a quick and easy marbling kit, lay out a piece of waxed paper and top with a layer of shaving cream. Smooth it out with a spatula. Sprinkle drops of ink on top of the shaving cream, then use a toothpick to swirl the ink into patterns. Slowly lay a piece of paper down on the ink and lift it up. Scrape the shaving cream off and reveal the pattern.

6" W x 4" H (15.24 x 10.16 cm)

SEND PAPER-CLOTH POSTCARDS

Fabric or paper-cloth postcards are small pieces of art that can be mailed like a postcard, traded with other artists, or even framed and given as gifts. They are 4" x 6" (10.16 x 15.24 cm), the same size as a standard paper postcard, and they can be sent through the U.S. mail. The United States Post Office has special rules that apply to "mail art," which are subject to change, so it's a good idea to consult with your local post office before you send anything. Since this is a fabric art, virtually any fabric technique can be applied, from quilting to embroidery. You also can use hand-dyed fabrics and even photos you've printed or transferred onto fabric.

CREATE PAPER POSTCARDS

1   Use the same collage principles shown for the other projects in this book. When your collage is finished, trim it to 4" x 6" (10.16 x 15.24 cm).

2   Cut a piece of plain or dyed cotton to 4" x 6" (10.16 x 15.24 cm) and adhere fusible web to the back.

3   Cut a piece of heavy stabilizer to 4" x 6" (10.16 x 15.24 cm) and iron the plain or dyed cotton fabric to it.

4   Use fabric glue to attach the paper-cloth collage to the front of the stabilizer.

5   Finish your postcard in one of several ways: Use a zigzag stitch on raw edges to finish. Finish with seam binding or fabric strips and top stitching. Use strips of paper-cloth to form a binding and top stitch.

6   On the back, draw a line down the center with permanent marker, then write "postcard" in the upper left corner.

7   If your postcard meets post office requirements, you can affix a stamp to it, and they will do the rest. Otherwise, encase it in a padded envelope for safety.

gallery

enJoy even moRE ways to woRk with paper-cloth

The delightful mischief created by the artists on the following pages makes it obvious that paper-cloth is adaptable to a wide variety of styles. These very special quilt and mixed-media artists each bring a unique perspective to the marriage of paper and cloth. You'll find whimsical quilts, painted fabrics, and the liberal use of ephemera in the work they so graciously share for your enjoyment. Whatever your skill level, you'll find something to inspire you here.

RECYCLED REMNANTS

The artist of this piece was inspired to go green and wanted to create something on a large scale using bits and pieces, extras, and found-object squares from old upholstery covers. She incorporated her love for metal, fabric, and paper as she rooted through all of her different stashes for the perfect objects to create the paper-cloth for this project. The thread used was going to be thrown away by the owner, but it was instead donated to the artist for the project. Hardly any glue was used as well—all of the elements were sewn together except in areas where she used fabric strips, such as the hangar bar, wood sticks, and the bells and circles hanging at the bottom.

13" W x 30" H (33.02 x 76.2 cm)
Paper-cloth, fabric, metal, found objects
with stitching
Belinda Spiwak

BANDANA SERIES POSTCARDS

Paper-cloth is perfect for doodling and such an easy surface to sew on. For this piece, the artist strove for contrast by outlining the mosaics in a contrasting color with a paint pen. The line going through the mosaic signifies the artist's independent thought when it comes to creating art—she does exactly what she wants to do in her very own way.

6" W x 4" H (15.24 x 10.16 cm)
Paper-cloth, buttons, paint pen
Belinda Spiwak

BEADED HEART

Just as I was inspired to create my own brand of paper-cloth through the techniques of Beryl Taylor, this artist also finds inspiration in Beryl. After taking a workshop with Beryl, this artist discovered that she enjoys using text and bold images to create her paper-cloth. This piece resulted from pure experimentation. The artist used some textured tissue paper and heavily doodled on the fabric paper. The gold edging is a simple technique using glue and a gold paint pen. In regard to sewing on the copper beads, patience is a virtue, the artist says.

6" W x 8" H (15.24 x 20.32 cm)
Paper-cloth, pen, gold paint pen, copper beads with sewing
Belinda Spiwak

BIRDS AND BEES

Papers, such as decorative wrapping papers and images scanned from a vintage children's book circa 1800 as well as green rice papers, were collaged onto fabric to create this paper-cloth. Once dry, the artist quilted it with wool batting. The areas without quilting are puffy and mimic trapunto quilting. The rest of the images were hand-rendered. The leathery image is actually a dark tea bag. The bag was left to dry for several days with the tea still inside. The brittleness and staining that resulted make it appear to be very old.

14" W x 14" H (35.56 x 35.56 cm)
Cotton, sewing pattern, vintage children's book page, unryu paper, wrapping paper, collage, textile paints, free-motion machine quilting, fabric
Judy Coates Perez

VERDIGRIS

This piece began as a collage of images that were printed onto white fabric and then highlighted with paint. Next, the artist drew simple floral designs over the painted surface and then painted the area around the designs green. The layers of color create depth within the design. Once dry, the fabric was fused to heavy interfacing. Panels were cut out and then stitched using a free-motion foot. Copper was sewn to the top edge and the sides were stitched together with satin stitching. To finish, the copper was embossed with a stylus.

7" W x 9" H x 4½" D (17.78 x 22.86 x 11.43 cm)
Printed paper images collaged with gel medium to cotton fabric and painted with textile paints
Judy Coates Perez

CYNARA CARDUNCULUS

"I like bringing incongruent materials like teabags, paper, paint, fabric, and metal together and sewing them into a piece of textile art," the artist says. "The images are random things that appeal to me, arranged in a pleasing layout." The background paper in this paper-cloth is actually a large tea bag, which the artist drew on with a permanent marker. The other paper used in the collage is plain white paper (copyright-free images were scanned and then printed on it). A mini Tarot card also was used. The fabric is cotton and was painted with textile paints. The image of the artichoke was glazed with several layers of transparent textile paint. The finished collage was fused to heavy interfacing and then quilted. To finish, the piece was trimmed in metal.

7½" W x 9" H (19.05 x 22.86 cm)
Large tea bag collaged on cotton fabric with markers, textile paint, aluminum, stitching, and embossing
Judy Coates Perez

DRESS

This piece evokes femininity and innocence. The dress is translucent and white with a lacy edge. The butterfly wings allude to new life, which females are able to bring forth. But the dress is also "stained," and the crimson streak running from the hem to the female pelvis below alludes to the idea that once a woman has given birth, she is no longer considered chaste. For this piece and the piece top right, the artist printed her own designs onto plain copy paper and then collaged and sewed them together. Spray glue was used to adhere the paper to fabric, then to felt, and the base layer of fabric. This was then free-motion stitched. The stitched quilt was slashed in places and restitched with a "ladder" of stitches over the cuts. When the stitching was complete, the entire quilt was painted with acrylic paints, gesso, and acrylic medium.

9½" W x 15½" H (24.13 x 39.37 cm)
Paper, fabric, felt, collage, stitch, paint
Carol Wiebe

HOME

Nothing is ever as simple as it seems. Home is about dreams, imagination, music, and light in the windows. But a crow flies over the roof, and there is no visible door on the house. To symbolize love, "x's" and "o's" are present, but there is also a "y," which intimates questions and ambiguity. "I work intuitively," Carol says, "putting patterns, images, and words together without conscious thought. Once those elements are combined, and I have everything sewn and quilted, I paint much the same way. When this creative flow diminishes, I stand back and analyze. I decide to change colors, block out one area, and collage something else over it, add an image or whatever comes to my mind."

13" W x 10" H (33.02 x 25.4 cm)
Paper, fabric, felt, collage, stitch, paint
Carol Wiebe

SWEET PEA

Sweet Pea is just that, a quilted and stitched version of pea pods and ten-drils, suggesting precious sustenance. The plant is rooted in the ground, but the artist has given it wings—such whimsical choices are an artist's pre-rogative. An entire piece of shaped felt was covered with tissue papier-mâché, and raised string designs were used for emphasis. The fabric stitched to this "background" was monoprinted with actual pods and then stitched by hand. When finished, it was attached to the papier-mâché with acrylic medium.

15½" W x 12" H (39.37 x 30.48 cm)
Fabric, felt, papier-mâché, stitch, paint
Carol Wiebe

GLOSSARY

ACRYLIC MEDIUM In mixed media, it serves as both a glue and a durable finish and is available in matte and gloss. This polymer emulsion can be used alone or mixed with acrylic paints.

ACRYLIC PAINTS These are some of the most versatile paints; they are composed of pigment in a synthetic base. Acrylics can be used in many formulas, from heavy-bodied to a wash, and they can be cleaned up with soap and water.

ALCOHOL INKS These permanent, transparent, and fast-drying inks can be used on any slick and nonporous surface, from glossy paper to metal and from plastic to glass. They blend well and allow for interesting mottled and polished stone effects.

ANGELINA A very fine, light-reflective fiber made from sheets. It can be ironed flat or molded to a stamp. It produces an iridescent effect.

ARTIST TRADING CARD Miniature artworks meant to be traded and collected. They are the size of a playing card, 2½" W × 3½" H (6.35 × 9 cm), and their canvas can be made of paper, card stock, fabric, metal, or glass.

AWL Used for punching holes, an awl is a tool with a long spike sharpened to a point.

BATTING A sheet of cotton, polyester, or wool, it forms the insulation between the top and backing layers of a quilt.

BEESWAX A natural wax produced by bees. It melts at 145° F and serves as a collage medium and coating material in mixed media.

BLEACH PEN Made by Clorox, it contains gel-formula bleach in a pen. Use it to draw on colored items, such as fabric or photos, to remove color and thereby create a design.

CARD STOCK This thick paper is used as cover sheets in mixed-media projects and in scrapbooking as the foundation of a scrapbook page. Card stock is usually 110 lb paper.

ENCAUSTIC WAX Composed of wax, pigment, and damar resin, it forms a harder finish than traditional beeswax, and it can be used in encaustic painting or as a collage medium.

EYELET SETTER Used to set small rings or eyelets for lacing into paper or fabric, this tool is made up of a metal rod with a special tip, which is hammered to set the eyelet.

EYELETS These small grommets can be set into paper or fabric. They have a functional side—use them to secure elements together or as lacing holes—or as design elements.

FABRIC GLUE Fabric glue is any white glue meant to adhere fabrics and porous materials, such as Delta Sobo Glue and Aleene's No Sew Fabric Glue by Duncan Enterprises.

FELT A fabric of compressed fibers, often made of wool, but also synthetic, it comes in a range of colors.

FELTING NEEDLE These specialty needles have a number of sharp barbs and an L-shaped handle; they are used for needlefelting roving into felt.

FIBERFILL This lightweight stuffing material made of synthetic fibers is used for filling dolls, pillows, and other sewn items.

FOIL For foiling fabric, it is available in sheets and in a variety of metallic colors. It is applied with fusible web or foil adhesive and ironed on to create a bright metallic finish.

FOIL GLUE An adhesive specially made for the application of fabric foil, it can be brushed or stamped on.

FREE-MOTION FOOT This transparent sewing-machine foot with a spring mechanism allows the needle to move in any direction and is used for sewing around shapes, quilting, and thread sketching.

FREEZER PAPER Freezer paper comes in rolls or sheets and can be used to stabilize fabric you wish to send through the printer. It has a special wax coating on one side that allows it to lightly and temporarily stick to other surfaces.

FUSIBLE WEB A fine mesh fiber that melts when heated, fusible web can be used between two layers of fabric to adhere them. Wonder Under and Stitch Witchery are popular brands. Fusible web is available with release paper backing.

GLUE STICK This is a solid adhesive paste in a twist-up tube.

GOLD LEAF PEN For projects that call for a golden touch, this gilding pen, such as Krylon 18k Gold Leafing Pen, contains a liquid metallic finish.

HEAT GUN Used for drying, melting, and embossing, this device emits a stream of hot air.

INK Ink is liquid containing pigment or dye and is used to color a surface or for writing with a pen or quill.

INK-JET FABRIC SHEETS These ready-to-print fabric sheets are stabilized, and the cotton, canvas, or silk fabric has been treated to accept ink. These will create permanent images when ironed.

INK-JET PRINTER The most common type of home printer, they propel semipermanent ink onto the page. Images are not waterproof unless pre-treated or coated.

INK PADS Also known as a rubber stamp pad, it is a small pad saturated with ink or dye, which is used with rubber stamps or for direct-to-paper inking techniques. They are available in several varieties: dye-based (not permanent), pigment-based (permanent), and solvent (permanent and allows for stamping on nonporous surfaces).

METAL TAPE This aluminum or copper foil backed with an adhesive comes in rolls of varying widths and thicknesses.

NONSTICK SHEET This heatproof pressing sheet for ironing will not stick to adhesives and will protect delicate materials from heat.

OIL PASTEL This is a wax oil crayon that goes on like a crayon, but it is highly pigmented.

PAINT MARKER This marker pen can be used to create permanent writing on a variety of surfaces.

PERMANENT MARKER For projects that incorporate wet media, use this waterproof pen to create marks on a variety of surfaces.

PHOTOCOPY When an image is made on a toner photocopier using a heat process, a photocopy is created. Toner photocopies are suitable for many mixed-media projects, including transfers.

ROTARY CUTTER This tool with a circular blade and a handle is used to cut fabric on a cutting mat.

ROVING A bundle of fibers ready to be spun into yarn, they can be made of wool, silk, soy, and corn.

SCREW PUNCH Otherwise known as a paper drill, this tool can punch holes through multiple layers of paper. It's used by bookbinders and mixed media artists.

STABILIZER Designed to support fabric under machine stitching, especially fabrics that are light-weight, it can also be used to stiffen sheets of fabric so that they can be run through a printer.

STRETCHED CANVAS Stretched on wooden bars and stapled, this is a paint-ready canvas. For mixed media, use gallery-wrapped canvas, which does not need to be framed.

TEXTIVA This iridescent sheet of film is cut to make Angelina. It shrinks when heated.

TRANSLUCENT LIQUID CLAY Used for tranfers, this polymer clay liquid becomes translucent and firm when heated.

ULTRA-THICK EMBOSSING ENAMEL This embossing powder has extra large particles, which form a hard, durable, glossy finish when melted.

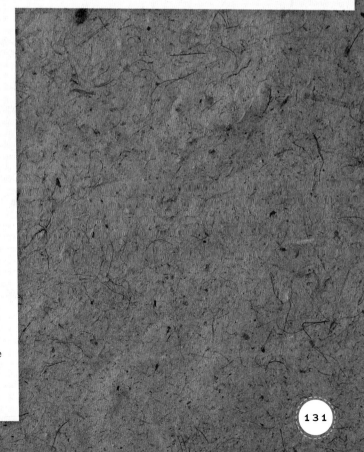

RESOURCES
PURVEYORS OF ARTSY POTIONS

quiltingartsllc.com
Books, roving, felting supplies, Paintstiks, felt, embroidery floss, angelina, fabric foil, stabilizer, ink-jet fabric sheets, fusible web, rubbing sheets

jeanettesfabrictodyefor.com
Luscious hand-dyed silks, cottons, velvets, and more

dharmatrading.com
Textile paints, dyes, transfer paper, bubble jet set, wax, stamp-carving supplies, brayers, printing plates, ink-jet fabric sheets, freezer paper, foam stamps, compressed sponge, markers, puff paint

dickblick.com
Stretched canvas, oil pastels, acrylic mediums, paints, stamp-carving supplies, rotary and craft cutters, cutting mats, inks, illustration board, beeswax, clay, fixatives, fabric crayons, paint markers, etc.

joann.com
Muslin, batting, notions, glue, clay, beads, art fibers, thread and sewing supplies, fabric dyes, markers, alcohol inks, stabilizer, fiberfill, fusible web, etc.

ARTISTS WHO INSPIRE

Melanie Testa – melanietesta.com
Denise Aumick – deniseaumick.com
Vickie Hallmark – vickiehallmark.com
Ann Johnston – annjohnston.net
Michelle Caplan – collagelab.blogspot.com
Denise Linet – deniselinet.com
Judy Wise – judywise.blogspot.com
Elaine Kerr – abstractionsart.blogspot.com
Dale Copeland – dalecopeland.co.nz

Melody Johnson – fibermania.blogspot.com
Nicole Tuggle – sigilation.com
Katie Kendrick – katiekendrick.com
Judy Coates Perez – judyperez.blogspot.com
Belinda Spiwak – alteredbelly.blogspot.com
Carol Wiebe – silverspringstudio.wordpress.com
Beryl Taylor – beryltaylor.com
Lisa Engelbrecht – lisaengelbrecht.com
Virginia Spiegel – virginiaspiegel.com

MANUFACTURERS OF MAGICKAL GOODS

AMERICAN ART CLAY COMPANY (AMACO)
amaco.com
Rub 'N Buff

DALER ROWNEY
daler-rowney.com
Artist's acrylic ink

DR. PH. MARTIN'S
docmartins.com
Bombay india ink

DUNCAN ENTERPRISES
duncancrafts.com
aleenes.com
Aleene's Tacky Glue & Aleene's
No Sew Glue

DYLON
dylon.co.uk
Dyes

ECLECTIC PRODUCTS
eclecticproducts.com
Craft Goop

SCHMINCKE
schmincke.de
TroCol Powder

SUZE WEINBERG
schmoozewithsuze.com
Ultra Thick Embossing
Enamel

GOLDEN ARTISTS COLORS
goldenpaints.com
Gel and matte medium

JACQUARD
jacquardproducts.com
Textile paints

KRYLON
krylon.com
Gold leafing pen

POLYFORM PRODUCTS
sculpey.com
Translucent liquid Sculpey

RANGER
rangerink.com
Alcohol and Adirondack inks
and color wash

RIT
ritdye.com
Dye

about the author

Kelli Nina Perkins is a public librarian with a master's degree in information and a self-taught mixed-media artist. She has always been inspired by the ephemera of everyday life, collecting and cataloging small treasures. Her work appears regularly in *Cloth Paper Scissors,* and she is a contributor to a number of books, including *Mixed-Media Self-Portraits: Inspiration & Techniques* by Cate Prato. She's taught soapmaking, paper beads, altered books, artist trading cards, and other arts throughout the Midwest and been a guest on the PBS show *Quilting Arts TV.* Kelli lives in Michigan with her amazing husband, colorful daughters, and a variety of entertaining pets. Visit her blog at ephemeralalchemy.blogspot.com.

contributors

BELINDA SPIWAK

Belinda Spiwak is a self-professed technique junkie and currently teaches found-object jewelry, collage, and background techniques. She works with fabric, collage, metal, beads, and found objects, repurposing everyday things in her mixed media. She is a sixth grade teacher and an avid blogger, sharing her art techniques with a wide audience. When she's not at her sewing machine or computer, she's in her suburban Chicago garage bending metal. Belinda writes for *Cloth Paper Scissors* and demonstrates techniques for Dremel. Visit her at alteredbelly.blogspot.com.

JUDY COATES PEREZ

Judy Coates Perez is an international award-winning textile artist who is well known for her highly detailed, colorfully painted whole-cloth quilts. She explores themes drawn from folklore, mythology, and nature, working in a variety of media. Often blending quilting skills with techniques drawn from her graphic-arts background, she uses textile paints, dyes, inks, acrylic powders, and artist's pencils on her fabric as well as sewing metal into her mixed-media pieces. Judy has written numerous articles for *Quilting Arts* and *Cloth Paper Scissors* magazines and has been a guest on the *Quilting Arts* PBS television program. Visit her at judyperez.blogspot.com.

CAROL WIEBE

Artist Carol Wiebe considers art to be a bridge from ordinary, everyday life to another country. She invites others to cross that bridge and enter into her country and experience a personal conversation. Carol is one of those people who became a teacher and a librarian through "practicality," but made art in every spare moment. At present, she is working part time and now that mixed-media paper quilts have been added to her repertoire, her passion has been ignited to a point where she risks spontaneous combustion! She resides in Canada. Visit her at silverspringstudio.com.

INDEX

acetone 57
acrylic ink 24
acrylic medium 130
acrylic paint 29, 130
alcohol ink 27, 130
angelina fiber 49, 62, 130, 131
appliqué 58–59; reverse 59
artist trading card 130
awl 130

batting 130
beading 65
beeswax 130
bleach pen 41, 111, 130
blotting 41
brayering paint 34
brushes 15
buttons 64

canvas 14; stretched 131
card stock 130
carved stamps 45
chalk 39
cloth 14; journal 68; layering 62; sheer 14
collagraph printing 53
color 21, 68; blotting 41; reducing 40; removing 40–41
color bleeding on paper 17
combing 32
construction, paper-cloth 10, 12
cotton 14
couching 59
crazy quilting 61
creativity exercises 71, 77, 93, 120
cutter, rotary 131

design elements 70

edges, ripped 55
eyelets 130
embellishments 64–65
embossing enamel 131
embossing resist 51
embroidery 60
enamel, embossing 131
encaustic wax 130
ephemera 13

fabric see cloth
felt 130
felting 60
felting needle 130
fiberfill 130
finishing 21
foam stamps 44
foils 56, 130
found objects 64
free-motion sewing machine foot 130
free-motion stitching 63, 98
freezer paper 15, 21, 130
fusible film 49
fusible web 130

gel 49
gesso 40
glazes 33
glue 15, 130; applying 17–18; mixing 17
glue guns 38
glue sticks 38, 130
gold leaf 37, 131
graffiti 55

heat gun 131

impasto 48
india ink 25
ink-jet printers 131; fabric sheets for 131
ink pads 131
inks 24–27, 131; blotting 25; dripping 26; spraying 25; stamping 26
inspiration, design 66–71; sources of 69
interfacing 14

journaling 63–65

kraft paper 12

lace printing 53
layering fabric 62
liquid clay 131

markers 39, 131
masking 50
metallics 35–38
metal powders 35
metal tape 111, 131
mica 36
mistakes 19
molding paste 47
monoprinting 52–53
mosaics 42
muslin 14

needlefelting 60
needles 98; felting 130

oil sticks 33, 131; metallic 38
opalescent paints 36

paint pens 29
paint-pen journaling 63
paints 29–38; interference 36; metallic

fabric 35; peeled 54; puff 48; techniques for applying 30–32; swatches 68
paint sticks 33, 38
paper 12–13; freezer 15, 21, 130; kraft tissue 12; miscellaneous 13; paste 47; recycled 13; waxed 47
paper preparation, sheet 16
paste, metallic wax 36; molding 47
paste paper 47
pens, bleach 41, 111, 130; paint 29, 131
Perez, Judy Coates 126, 127
photocopy 131
photos 68, altered 56
pressing sheet 131
puff paint 48
pulling paint 30

quilting 61; crazy 61

ragging paint 34
recycled paper 13
resists 50–51; embossing 51; wax 51
rotary cutter 131
roving 131
rust embossing 55

scraping paint 31
screw punch 131
serendipity squares 42
sewing machines 98
shimmer spray 37
size of artwork 98
spackle 48
Spiwak, Belinda 123, 124, 125

splattering paint 29
sponge stamps 45
sponging paint 31
stabilizer 14, 131
stains 24; coffee and tea 28
stamping 43–45, 64; over- 43; white 44
stamps, carved 45; foam 44; sponge 45
stapling 65
stenciling 52
stencils, letter 111
stitching, contrast 59; free-motion 63, 98
surfaces for stitching 98
swatches, paint 68

tape 49; metal 111, 131
tape transfers 57
Textiva 131
texture 18, 46–49
threads 98
thread sketching 63, 98
tissue paper 12–13, 18
traction 98
transfers 57

undercoat 40

walnut ink 28
watercolor paints 32
waxed paper 46
wax, encaustic 130
wax paste, metallic 36
wax resist 51
webbing, spray 46
Wiebe, Carol 128, 129

create inspiring designs
WITH THESE RESOURCES FROM INTERWEAVE

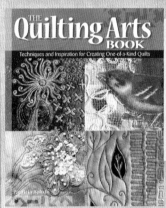